Memorizing God's Word: ™ *HIStory* (KJV)

Seeing Jesus in Genesis Chapter One

R. M. Lewis

WestBow
PRESS
A DIVISION OF THOMAS NELSON

WestBow Press books may be ordered through booksellers or by contacting:

WestBow Press
A Division of Thomas Nelson
1663 Liberty Drive
Bloomington, IN 47403
www.westbowpress.com
1-(866) 928-1240

Because of the dynamic nature of the Internet, any web addresses or links contained in this book may have changed since publication and may no longer be valid. The views expressed in this work are solely those of the author and do not necessarily reflect the views of the publisher, and the publisher hereby disclaims any responsibility for them.

ISBN: 978-1-4497-1489-5 (sc)

Library of Congress Cataloguing-in-Publication Data 2011925478

Scripture quotations are taken from The Holy Bible:, King James Version (KJV)

Cover concept and illustration by R. M. Lewis. All rights reserved.

The FLOW Coding Method is a trademark registered in the United States Patent and Trademark Offices by R. M. Lewis. savingfaith2011@gmail.com

Printed in the United States of America

WestBow Press rev. date: 3/24/2011

*This book is dedicated to all the pastors
and Bible teachers in my life from infancy.*

*It also is dedicated to publishers who
meticulously preserve the sacred trust of
word for word translations of the Holy Bible
from reliable copies of ancient manuscripts.
Without word for word translations, I could
not have written this book.*

*A special thank you to Joyce Strickland
and Janet Norman for editorial services.*

*I thank my family and my prayer partner –
best friends who enrich my life with prayer,
support, and joy.*

*To my prayer partner – best friends, what
a joyous time being with you at my 40th
wedding anniversary! Some of you were
present for the 25th celebration, but this
time was exceptional with the effort of
country-wide travel and your wonderful
testimonies enjoyed by so many loved ones.*

*Above all my love, devotion, and adulation
to my Savior and Lord Jesus Christ for
without abiding in You, I am nothing.*

CONTENTS
King James Version

I. SEEING JESUS IN CREATION: THE QUEST

My fascination with "Seeing Jesus in Creation" began more than twelve years ago. It began with a question of why did God bless the entirety of Creation as "good," but did not include "it was good" on the second day.

I read other reliable word for word Bible translations and "good" was definitely not there for Creation Day Two. It was also noteworthy that "the light" on Creation Day One was different from the "lights made" on Creation Day Four.

My curiosity was energized as to why? Was there an analogy related to the omission of "good" on the second day, and the distinction between the light on the first day of Creation and the lights on Day Four? Those two facts were so exciting to ponder as I read the Bible and listen to Scriptures.

I made an elementary sketch of the days of Creation early one morning, because after midnight I would study the Bible and meditate. That was my time with God in silence without interruption.

Subsequent drawings were made after my first one shredded from frequent use. The date of a later sketch is January 12, 1999.

When a particular Scripture was illuminated, I would be ecstatic. Scripture references, notes, and additional details would be added to the sketch.

It seemed reasonable that if there was an analogy, it could only be about the ministry of Jesus. My mind was intrigued with the hope of seeing Jesus in Creation.

The quest was on with exuberance. My lifestyle of reading the Bible from cover to cover took on a new intensity as I searched for Jesus. The front cover of this book is designed from the old drawings from 1999.

The collection of Bible verses in this book represent more than a decade of pondering with God usually between the hours of 1:30 a.m. to 3:30 a.m. and/or 3:00 a.m. to 5 a.m. This was supreme private time with God, and it still thrills me.

"Seeing Jesus in Creation" is an analogy; it is not theological doctrine. It is merely my perspective of viewing Scriptures about Jesus and the church through the narrative of Genesis Chapter One.

This book has a dual purpose. My first purpose is to share some interesting insights from God's work in Creation and Jesus' work on earth. My second purpose is to demonstrate the FLOW Coding Method ® for memorizing God's Word.

My hope is that you enjoy the scriptural narrative about Jesus Christ which dovetails Bible verses from Genesis Chapter One into a synopsis of HIStory. After reading the next page, please proceed to page 25, the Analogy Overview.

Back pages are intentionally left blank except for analogy pages.

Seeing Jesus in Creation: Creator God

Is it possible to see the Lord Jesus Christ in Genesis Chapter One? Are there Bible verses about the earthly ministry of Jesus Christ that could be interwoven into Days One through Seven?

The Holy Bible from Genesis to Revelation declares HIStory, but in particular in Genesis Chapter One, there are dovetailing Bible verses for:
Day 1: Knowing Him / Foundation
Day 2: Saving Faith / Salvation
Day 3: Standing Secure / Assurance
Day 4: Becoming Christlike / Transformation
Day 5: Glorifying God / Maturation
Day 6: Anticipating Heaven / Kingdom, and
Day 7: Living Hope / Meditation.

"The Quest" on page 9 summarizes how this search began. The analogy of Genesis Chapter One, "Seeing Jesus in Creation," is in the Resource of Scriptures. It begins on page 25. The Holy Bible declares:

1. The Word was with God, and the Word was God. The same [Jesus] was in the beginning with God.   John 1:1b,2

2. And he is before all things, and by him all things consist.   Col. 1:17

3. For by him were all things created, that are in heaven, and that are in earth, visible and invisible, whether they be thrones, or dominions, or principalities, or powers: all things were created by him, and for him:
                   Col. 1:16

4. And he is the head of the body, the church ... the firstborn from the dead; that in all things he might have the preeminence.   Col. 1:18

5. All things were made by him; and without him was not any thing made that was made.
                   John 1:3

6. For it pleased the Father that in him should all fulness dwell; And, having made peace through the blood of his cross, by him to reconcile all things unto himself ... whether they be things in earth, or things in heaven. Col. 1:19,20

7. In this was manifested the love of God toward us, because that God sent his only begotten Son into the world, that we might live through him.   1 John 4:9

8. For he hath made him to be sin for us, who knew no sin; that we might be made the righteousness of God in him.   2 Cor. 5:21

9. For there is one God, and one mediator between God and men, the man Christ Jesus; Who gave himself a ransom for all, to be testified in due time.   1 Tim. 2:5,6

The tool for memorizing Scriptures of HIStory in this book, is the FLOW Coding Method ®. This system is an easy tool that immediately and successfully works. It is basically a two-part process: (1) visualizing a Bible verse in phrases, and (2) Coding or writing the first letter of each word in the phrase. "FLOW" is an acronym for:

*F*irst
*L*etter
*O*f
*W*ord™.

This book explains in detail how to use the FLOW Method™. Depending on the verse, an already coded Bible verse takes five minutes to memorize. Once memorized, the Holy Spirit can illuminate that Scripture in your heart at anytime. **Please proceed to page 25, the Analogy Overview.**

II.   DEMONSTRATING THE FLOW CODING METHOD ®
The Nine Steps

1.   Ask God to help you.
Pray for His help in understanding and in memorizing the Scripture.

2.   Read aloud the verse.
Use your senses of **seeing, speaking**, and **hearing** to stimulate your memory.

Unformatted Verse Example:

John 3:17
For God sent not his Son into the world to condemn the world; but that the world through him might be saved.

3.   Visualize writing the verse in phrases using a separate line for each phrase.
Observe how to divide the verse into short, comfortable phrases.

4.   Write the verse in Phrase-format with its address before and after the verse.
A verse can be formatted into phrases by concepts, natural pauses of thought, punctuation, and by placing difficult to remember words on a separate line.

Phrase-formatted Verse Example:

John 3:17
For God sent not his Son
into the world
to condemn the world;   but that
the world through him
might be saved.
                                    John 3:17

---

5.   Code the Phrase-formatted verse by writing the first letter of each word.
FLOW is the acronym for Coding or writing the *F*irst *L*etter *O*f each *W*ord.

Leave a blank line to prompt your memory for the second address or reference.

FLOW Coded Verse Example:

John 3:17
F G s n h S
i t w
t c t w;   b t
t w t h
m b s.
Address____

---

6.   Read aloud the Phrase-formatted verse with its address three or more times. PAUSE after each line.
Read with emphasis or repeat a difficult to remember phrase three times. For example, read aloud three times:
"... to condemn the world;   but that ... "

7.   Use the Code to say aloud the verse with its address three or more times.
Repeat difficult lines three or more times. Look back at the words as needed. If you keep forgetting certain words, re-read aloud the Phrase-formatted verse several times before using the Code again. For example:

John 3:17
F G s n h S   (repeat three times)
i t w   (recite with emphasis)
t c t w;   b t (repeat three times)
t w t h   (recite with emphasis)
m b s.   (recite with emphasis)
Address____

8.   Recite aloud the verse from memory while visualizing the Code.

9.   Thank God for helping you. Review often with the Code first, then the verse.

III. MEMORIZING TIPS

1. If a verse is already Phrase-formatted™ and Coded, use a half sheet of paper to cover the Code, or glue the verse to an index card, and use the reverse side for the Code. **Read the verse out loud three times. Pause after each line**.

2. When Phrase-formatting™ a verse, use large type, and write the Scripture reference or address before and after the verse(s). Read aloud the reference/address each time.

3. When Coding a verse, leave the second address line blank to prompt your memory for the reference. Say the reference out loud.

4. When memorizing consecutive verses, write the reference number beside each verse if you like.

5. As needed, also number the lines (1, 2, 3, etc.) to prevent skipping a line as you practice.

6. When Phrase-formatting™, look for patterns in a verse, for example, repeated concepts, words, parts of speech, etc.

7. Experiment with memory prompts: spacial alignments within a line, indentation for various parts of speech, italics, color-coding, bold print, and underlining.

8. If a verse is difficult to remember, Phrase-format™ the Scripture with more memory prompts. Also in rapid succession, repeat three times or recite with emphasis any forgotten line. As you use the FLOW Coding Method ®, customize your prompts.

9. Memory prompts that can be used to enhance memorization are: shorter Phrase-formatted™ lines and spacial alignments.

10. If a Bible translation does not capitalize the pronouns referring to God, consider bold print, underlining, or color-coding **His** pronouns to increase comprehension.

11. At the end of a line if you triple space before the conjunction "and" as well as the pronoun "that", it will prompt your memory for the next word. The same could be done for other conjunctions if you so desire.

12. Possessive words could be coded with 's. For example, "those who are Christ's" is coded as "t w a C's." Keep the punctuation of hyphens and dashes. For example, "I – My" is coded as "I – M."

Isaiah 45:12a	Is. 45:12a
I have made the earth, And	I h m t e, A
created man on it.	c m o i.
I – My hands –	I – M h –
stretched out	s o
the heavens,	t h,
Is. 45:12a (NKJV)	Addr.____

13. To enhance retention, observe the first word of each Phrase-formatted™ line, and read aloud three times the sequence of first words. Please refer to the verse above and speak: **I, created, I – My, stretched, the.** Now read the Phrase-formatted™ verse.

14. When reading or reciting Bible verses, remember to: **Speak out loud at least three times, and PAUSE after each line.**

IV. MASTERING LONG PASSAGES

1. Read aloud the entire passage of Bible verses for understanding.

2. Re-read aloud the passage noting the natural flow of concepts, words, and parts of speech for Phrase-formatting™ the verses. If possible, use only one line for each verse.

3. Divide the passage into groups of verses. Memorize one group then recite from the beginning before memorizing the next group.

4. Consider using bold print, underlining, or color-coding for references to God. For example: "**to the Lord**" and "**His name.**"

5. Use *italics* for verbs. This will prompt your memory that a *verb* comes next.

6. With a lengthy passage, use additional lines and spaces only as needed. Write the reference number beside each Bible verse. **Read out loud. PAUSE after each line.**

7. When a verse is difficult to remember, practice repeating three times and/or reciting with emphasis a line. For example:

Isaiah 45:18

For thus saith the LORD	that (with emphasis)
created the heavens;	(with emphasis)
God himself	that (with emphasis)
formed the earth ...	(with emphasis)
I am the LORD;	and (with emphasis)
there is none else.	(repeat three times)
Is. 45:18	

Isaiah 45:18

F t st L t	(with emphasis)
c t h;	(with emphasis)
G h, t	(with emphasis)
f t e ...	(with emphasis)
I a t L; a	(with emphasis)
t i n e.	(repeat three times)
Address____	

8. Create a Memory Barcode prompt at the top of long passages. Please refer to below and "Practicing What You Have Learned."

Memory Barcode™ Phrase-formatted Example

Note: At the top of the group of verses below is a Memory Barcode; it lists verse reference numbers **6,7,** and **8**, and the first letter of each verse and its subordinate line(s). The Scripture below is formatted to have references to **God in bold print**, and *verbs* and some *adverbs* in *italics*. The letters in the Memory Barcode retain the capitalization, bold print, and italics of the first letter of each line. (Psalm 33:6-14 is on page 21.)

Psalm 33:6-8

6   7   8

Ba Hh *Ll*

6 **By the word of the LORD** *were* the heavens *made*;
   and all the host of them **by the breath of his mouth.**

7 **He** *gathereth* the waters of the sea together as an heap:
   he *layeth up* the depth in storehouses.

8 *Let* all the earth *fear* **the LORD:**
   let all the inhabitants of the world *stand* **in awe of him.**

FLOW Coded™

6   7   8

Ba Hh *Ll*

6 **B t w o t L** *w* t h *m*,
   a a t h o t **b t b o h m.**

7 **H** *g* t w o t s t a a h:
   h *l u* t d i s.

8 *L* a t e *f t* **L:**
   l a t i o t w *s i a o h.*

V.   PRACTICING WHAT YOU HAVE LEARNED

(Be **doers** of the 9 Steps)

A. SHORT VERSE UNFORMATTED EXAMPLE:

Who is the image of the invisible God, the firstborn of every creature: Colossians 1:15

Phrase-formatted™	**FLOW Coded**™
Colossians 1:15	Colossians 1:15
[Jesus] Who is the image	W i t i
of the invisible God,	o t i G,
the firstborn of every creature:	t f o e c:
Col. 1:15	Addr._____

B. MORE DIFFICULT VERSE UNFORMATTED EXAMPLE:

For the invisible things of him from the creation of the world are clearly seen, being understood by the things that are made, even his eternal power and Godhead; so that they are without excuse: Romans 1:20

Phrase-formatted™ **by Punctuation**	**FLOW Coded**™
Romans 1:20	Romans 1:20
For the invisible things of **him** from the creation of the world are clearly seen,	F t i t o **h** f t c o t w a c s,
being understood by the things that are made,	b u b t t t a m,
even **his** eternal power and Godhead;	e **h** e p a G;
so that they are without excuse:	s t t a w e:
Rom. 1:20	Addr._____

Phrase-formatted™ **by Thought Pauses**	**FLOW Coded**™
Romans 1:20	Romans 1:20
For the invisible things of **him** from the creation of the world	F t i t o **h** f t c o t w
are clearly seen,	a c s,
being understood by the things that are made,	b u b t t t a m,
even **his** eternal power and Godhead;	e **h** e p a G;
so that they are without excuse:	s t t a w e:
Rom. 1:20	Addr._____

Phrase-formatted™ **with Memory Prompts**		**FLOW Coded**™	
Romans 1:20		Romans 1:20	
For the invisible things of **him**		F t i t o **h**	
from the creation of the world		f t c o t w	
are clearly seen,		a c s,	
being understood by the things	that	b u b t t	t
are made,		a m,	
even **his** eternal power	and	e **h** e p	a
Godhead;	so that	G;	s t
they are without excuse:		t a w e:	
Rom. 1:20		Addr._____	

Practicing What You Have Learned
(Be **doers** of the 9 Steps)

C. LONG PASSAGE UNFORMATTED EXAMPLE:

Psalm 33:6-14

6 By the word of the LORD were the heavens made; and all the host of them by the breath of his mouth.

7 He gathereth the waters of the sea together as an heap: he layeth up the depth in storehouses.

8 Let all the earth fear the LORD: let all the inhabitants of the world stand in awe of him.

9 For he spake, and it was done; he commanded, and it stood fast.

10 The LORD bringeth the counsel of the heathen to nought: he maketh the devices of the people of none effect.

11 The counsel of the LORD standeth for ever, the thoughts of his heart to all generations.

12 Blessed is the nation whose God is the LORD; and the people whom he hath chosen for his own inheritance.

13 The LORD looketh from heaven; he beholdeth all the sons of men.

14 From the place of his habitation he looketh upon all the inhabitants of the earth.

Memory Barcode™ Phrase-formatted Passage
Psalm 33:6-14

6	7	8	9	10	11	12	13	14
Ba	Hh	*Ll*	Fh	Th	Tt	Ba	Th	Fh

6 **By the word of the LORD** *were* the heavens *made*;
and all the host of them **by the breath of his mouth**.

7 **He** *gathereth* the waters of the sea together as an heap:
he *layeth up* the depth in storehouses.

8 *Let* all the earth *fear* **the LORD:**
let all the inhabitants of the world *stand* **in awe of him.**

9 For **he** *spake*, and it *was done*;
he *commanded*, and it *stood* fast.

10 **The LORD** *bringeth* the counsel of the heathen to nought:
he *maketh* the devices of the people of none effect.

11 **The counsel of the LORD** *standeth* for ever,
the thoughts of his heart to all generations.

12 Blessed *is* the nation whose **God** *is* **the LORD;**
and the people whom **he** *hath chosen* **for his own inheritance.**

13 **The LORD** *looketh* from heaven;
he *beholdeth* all the sons of men.

14 From the place **of his habitation**
he *looketh upon* all the inhabitants of the earth.
Ps. 33:6-14

FLOW Coded™
Psalm 33:6-14

6	7	8	9	10	11	12	13	14
Ba	Hh	*Ll*	Fh	Th	Tt	Ba	Th	Fh

6 **B t w o t L** *w* t h *m*,
a a t h o t **b** t **b o H m.**

7 **H** *g* t w o t s t a a h:
h *l u* t d i s.

8 *L* a t e *f* t **L:**
l a t i o t w *s* i a **o h.**

9 F **h** *s*, a i *w d*;
h *c*, a i s f.

10 **T L** *b* t c o t h t n:
h *m* t d o t p o n e.

11 **T c o t L** *s* f e,
t t o h h t a g.

12 B i t n w **G** *i* t **L;**
a t p w **h** *h c* **f h o i.**

13 **T L** *l* f h;
h *b* a t s o m.

14 F t p **o h h**
h *l u* a t i o t e.
Addr._____

VI.   RESOURCE OF FLOW CODED™ SCRIPTURES: OVERVIEWS

FLOW OVERVIEW

The Scriptures in this section are a narrative of God's work at Creation and Christ's work on earth. The Bible verses are formatted for memorization using the FLOW Coding Method ®.

In this Resource of FLOW Coded™ Scriptures, the Scriptures for each day of Creation are interwoven with corresponding Bible verses. For the pure delight of the Word of God, first read the Scriptures, then experiment with the method.

Effective helps and suggestions for using the method are included in the chapters on: Demonstrating the FLOW Coding Method ®; Memorizing Tips; Mastering Long Passages; and Practicing What You Have Learned.

If you follow the instructions in the above sections, you have the tools to implement the FLOW Method™ and to enjoy how it works. There is no exact way of using the technique. If you have a better method of coding Scripture, use it.

After reading the Resource of Scriptures section, select your own verses to be memorized. For a quick start, use a half sheet of paper to cover the Code, or fold a two-column page in this section of the book and begin practicing. You will enjoy the results.

ANALOGY OVERVIEW

Analogy: a partial likeness between two things that are compared. The following analogies view the Scriptures about Jesus and the church through Genesis Chapter One. The first page of each Analogy is the synopsis. The second page is the Genesis account for that day of Creation and the correlation. The pages following the Analogy have corresponding Bible verses interwoven with the Genesis account. I have highlighted, "God said that it was good."

Creation	God's Work at Creation	Jesus' Work on Earth	Analogy
DAY 1	The Light	Incarnation	Page 27, 28
DAY 2	Firmament / Expanse	Crucifixion	Page 39, 40
DAY 3	Earth and Vegetation	Burial and Resurrection	Page 59, 60
DAY 4	Lights	Witnesses	Page 71, 72
DAY 5	Fish and Birds	Great Commission and Pentecost	Page 85, 86
DAY 6	Adam and His Bride	Christ and His Bride	Page 101, 102
DAY 7	God Rested	Jesus Christ Rested	Page 121, 122

DAY ONE: ANALOGY SYNOPSIS

On Creation Day One,
God's work in Creation was to send a unique light.

This reminds me of God the Father sending Jesus,
the true Light to the world.

ANALOGY: CREATION DAY ONE

Analogy: a partial likeness between two things that are compared. This analogy seeks to view the Scriptures about Jesus and the church through the narrative of Genesis Chapter One.

Creation Day 1: Genesis 1:1-5

1 In the beginning God created the heaven and the earth. 2 And the earth was without form, and void; and darkness was upon the face of the deep. And the Spirit of God moved upon the face of the waters. 3 And God said, Let there be light: and there was light. 4 And God saw the light, that it was good: and God divided the light from the darkness. 5 And God called the light Day, and the darkness he called Night. And the evening and the morning were the first day.

God's Work in Creation: God said, "Let there be light." Light is given or sent.

Jesus' Work on Earth: Incarnation: God the Father gave Jesus, the true Light, to the world.

Bible Verse Keywords: Light; true Light; life; I must work; day star; the bright and morning star; light is sprung up; And God saw the light, that it was good:

Pondered: 1. The Holy Bible is replete with Scriptures proclaiming that the world was made "by", "for", "in", and "through" Jesus Christ. Please refer to "Seeing Jesus in Creation: Creator God" on page 11.

2. The lights on Creation Day Four are made. Note the distinction between the "made lights" on Creation Day Four from "the light" on Day One.
Creation Day Four:
Genesis 1:14 And God said, Let there be lights in the firmament of the heaven to divide the day from the night; and let them be for signs, and for seasons, and for days, and years: 15 And let them be for lights in the firmament of the heaven to give light upon the earth: and it was so. 16 And God made two great lights; the greater light to rule the day, and the lesser light to rule the night: he made the stars also. 17 And God set them in the firmament of the heaven to give light upon the earth, 18 And to rule over the day and over the night, and to divide the light from the darkness: and God saw that it was good. 19 And the evening and the morning were the fourth day.
Creation Day One:
Genesis 1:3 And God said, Let there be light: and there was light. 4 And God saw the light, that it was good: and God divided the light from the darkness. 5 And God called the light Day, and the darkness He called Night. And the evening and the morning were the first day.

3. On Creation Days Three through Six, the Bible declares, "And God saw that it was good." Only on Creation Day One, does God identify "it." The Scripture heralds, "And God saw the light, that it was good ... ."

4. Could it be that this unique "light" is an analogy of Jesus, the "true Light," the beloved Son of God, in Whom Father God is well pleased?

DAY 1:   KNOWING HIM

1.   Genesis 1:1,2
In the beginning God created
the heaven   and the earth.   And
the earth was without form,   and
void;   and darkness was
upon the face of the deep.   And
the Spirit of God moved
upon the face of the waters.
Gen. 1:1,2

1.   Genesis 1:1,2
I t b G c
t h   a t e. A
t e w w f,   a
v;   a d w
u t f o t d.   A
t S o G m
u t f o t w.
Addr.____

2.   Genesis 1:3
And God said,
Let there be light: and
there was light.
Gen. 1:3

2.   Genesis 1:3
A G s,
L t b l: a
t w l.
Addr.____

3.   John 1:9
That was the true Light [Jesus],
which lighteth
every man   that
cometh into the world.
Jn. 1:9

3.   John 1:9
T w t t L,
w l
e m   t
c i t w.
Addr.____

4.   John 3:16
For God so loved the world,   that
he gave
his only begotten Son,   that
whosoever believeth in **him** [Jesus]
should not perish,   but
have everlasting life.
Jn. 3:16

4.   John 3:16
F G s l t w, t
h g
h o b S,   t
w b i **h**
s n p,   b
h e l.
Addr.____

5.   1 Thessalonians 5:9
For God hath not appointed us
to wrath,   but
to obtain salvation
by
our Lord Jesus Christ,
1 Thess. 5:9

5.   1 Thessalonians 5:9
F G h n a u
t w, b
t o s
b
o L J C,
Addr.____

6.   Acts 4:12
Neither is there salvation
in any other:
for there is none other name
under heaven ...
whereby we must be saved.
Acts 4:12

7.   Hebrews 2:14
Forasmuch then
as the children
are partakers of
flesh and blood,
[Jesus] **he** also **himself** likewise
took part of the same;   that
through death
he might destroy him   that
had the power of death,
that is, the devil;
Heb. 2:14

8.   1 Corinthians 15:21
For since by man [Adam]
came death,
by **man** [Jesus] came
also the resurrection
of the dead.
1 Cor. 15:21

9.   John 1:4
In **him** was life;   and
the life was
the light of men.
Jn. 1:4

10.   Colossians 2:9
For in **him** dwelleth
all the fulness
of the Godhead   bodily.
Col. 2:9

6.   Acts 4:12
N i t s
i a o:
f t i n o n
u h ...
w w m b s.
Addr.____

7.   Hebrews 2:14
F t
a t c
a p o
f a b,
h a **h** l
t p o t s; t
t d
h m d h   t
h t p o d,
t i, t d;
Addr.____

8.   1 Corinthians 15:21
F s b m
c d,
b **m** c
a t r
o t d.
Addr.____

9.   John 1:4
I **h** w l;   a
t l w
t l o m.
Addr.____

10.   Colossians 2:9
F i **h** d
a t f
o t G   b.
Addr.____

11. John 14:6	11. John 14:6
Jesus saith ... I am	J s ... I a
the way,	t w,
the truth, and	t t, a
the life:	t l:
no man cometh	n m c
unto the Father, but	u t F, b
by **me**.	b **m**.
Jn. 14:6	Addr._____

12. John 12:46; Luke 2:32	12. John 12:46; Luke 2:32
I am come a light	I a c a l
into the world, that	i t w, t
whosoever believeth on **me**	w b o **m**
should not abide in darkness. Luke 2:32	s n a i d.
A light to lighten	A l t l
the Gentiles, and	t G, a
the glory of ... Israel.	t g o ... I.
Jn. 12:46; Lk. 2:32	Addr._____

13. Acts 26:18	13. Acts 26:18
To open their eyes, and	T o t e, a
to turn them	t t t
from darkness to light, and	f d t l, a
from the power of Satan	f t p o S
unto God, that	u G, t
they may receive	t m r
forgiveness of sins, and	f o s, a
inheritance among them which are sanctified	i a t w a s
by faith that is in **me**.	b f t i i **m**.
Acts 26:18	Addr._____

14. Romans 1:20a	14. Romans 1:20a
For the invisible things of **him**	F t i t o **h**
from the creation of the world	f t c o t w
are clearly seen,	a c s,
being understood by the things that	b u b t t t
are made,	a m,
even **his** eternal power and Godhead;	e **h** e p a G;
Rom. 1:20a	Addr._____

15.   John 9:4
[Jesus said] I must work
the works of **him**   that
sent **me**,
while it is day:
the night cometh,
when no man can work.
Jn. 9:4

15.   John 9:4
I m w
t w o **h**   t
s **m**,
w i i d:
t n c,
w n m c w.
Addr.____

16.   Luke 1:78,79
Through the tender mercy
of our God;
whereby the dayspring
from on high
hath visited us,
To give light to them   that
sit in darkness   and
in the shadow of death,
to guide our feet
into the way of peace.
Lk. 1:78,79

16.   Luke 1:78,79
T t t m
o o G;
w t d
f o h
h v u,
T g l t t   t
s i d   a
i t s o d,
t g o f
i t w o p.
Addr.____

17.   John 16:33a
These things I have spoken
unto you,   that in **me** [Jesus]
ye might have peace.
Jn. 16:33a

17.   John 16:33a
T t I h s
u y,   t i **m**
y m h p.
Addr.____

18.   2 Peter 1:19
We have also
a more sure word of prophecy;
whereunto ye do well   that
ye take heed,
as unto a light   that
shineth in a dark place,
until the day dawn,   and
the day star arise
in your hearts:
2 Pet. 1:19

18.   2 Peter 1:19
W h a
a m s w o p;
w y d w   t
y t h,
a u a l   t
s i a d p,
u t d d,   a
t d s a
i y h:
Addr.____

19.   Revelation 22:16
I Jesus ...
I am the root   and
the offspring of David,   and
the bright   and morning star.
Rev. 22:16

19.   Revelation 22:16
I J ...
I a t r   a
t o o D,   a
t b   a m s.
Addr.____

20.   Matthew 4:16
The people
which sat in darkness
saw great light;   and
to them which sat
in the region   and
shadow of death
light is sprung up.
Mt. 4:16

20.   Matthew 4:16
T p
w s i d
s g l;   a
t t w s
i t r   a
s o d
l i s u.
Addr.____

21.   Matthew 4:17
From that time
Jesus began to preach,   and to say,
Repent:
for the kingdom of heaven
is at hand.
Mt. 4:17

21.   Matthew 4:17
F t t
J b t p,   a t s,
R:
f t k o h
i a h.
Addr.____

22.   Genesis 1:4
And God saw   the light,   that
it was good: and
God divided the light
from the darkness.
Gen. 1:4

22.   Genesis 1:4
A G s   t l,   t
i w g: a
G d t l
f t d.
Addr.____

23.   Genesis 1:5
And God called the light Day,   and
the darkness he called Night.   And
the evening   and the morning
were the first day.
Gen. 1:5

23.   Genesis 1:5
A G c t l D,   a
t d h c N.   A
t e   a t m
w t f d.
Addr.____

DAY TWO: ANALOGY SYNOPSIS

On Creation Day Two,
God's work in Creation was to create firmament –
the air or expanse between heaven and earth.

This reminds me of the crucifixion of Jesus. He was
nailed to the cross and lifted up from the earth. His
death occurred in the air between heaven and earth.

ANALOGY: CREATION DAY TWO

Analogy: a partial likeness between two things that are compared. This analogy is seeking to view the Scriptures about Jesus and the church through the narrative of Genesis Chapter One.

___

Creation Day 2:   Genesis 1:6-8

6 And God said, Let there be a firmament in the midst of the waters, and let it divide the waters from the waters. 7 And God made the firmament, and divided the waters which were under the firmament from the waters which were above the firmament: and it was so. 8 And God called the firmament Heaven. And the evening and the morning were the second day.

God's Work in Creation: God created firmament or expanse/space/air.

Jesus' Work on Earth: Crucifixion: God's penalty of death for sin is paid.

Bible Verse Keywords: Firmament; the firmament Heaven; prince of the power of the air; spiritual wickedness in high places; the devil is come down; serpent; devil; death; (Note: Although Satan is prince of the power of the air, Jesus is King and Lord of all.) Crucify Him; Crucify Him. *Please note the horrific details of the words said, and the deeds done to Jesus prior to His murder.* If thou shalt confess with thy mouth the Lord Jesus, and shalt believe in ... .

Pondered: 1. "That it was good" is not included in Creation Day Two – the shortest of all the Creation accounts. This curious fact energized my quest of looking for Jesus in Creation. See "The Quest" on page 9.

2. The Bible states in Ephesians 2:2: "the prince of the power of the air" is Satan. The air is the expanse above the surface of the earth. Reference Job 1:6,7: "Now there was a day when the sons of God came to present themselves before the LORD, and Satan came also among them. And the LORD said unto Satan, Whence comest thou? Then Satan answered the LORD ... , From going to and fro in the earth ... ." Satan is the prince of the power of the air. See "How to be Saved" on page 129.

3. Jesus was crucified in the air. He was lifted up on the cross and hung there until He died. God, His Father, laid His judgement of sin on His Son.

4. The innocent Son chose to do His Father's will. He bore all the sins of the entire world upon His sinless Self before His Holy Father. Jesus said, "Now is the judgment of this world: now shall the prince of this world be cast out. And I, if I be lifted up from the earth, will draw all men unto me"– John12:31,32. Jesus' work on the cross conquered Satan's power.

5. Jesus was reviled, mocked, spat upon, and tortured by the very humans He created. Then came His anguished separation from His Holy Father.

6. Could it be that Day Two – the shortest account of Creation, in some respect, relates to the inclination for that torturous day to end quickly?

DAY 2:   SAVING FAITH

SALVATION SCRIPTURES

1.   Genesis 1:6-8a
And God said,
Let there be a firmament
    in the midst of the waters,   and
    let it divide the waters
    from the waters.   And
God made the firmament,   and
    divided the waters
    which were under the firmament
    from the waters
    which were above the firmament: and
    it was so.   And
God called the firmament Heaven.
Gen. 1:6-8a

1.   Genesis 1:6-8a
A G s,
L t b a f
    i t m o t w, a
    l i d t w
    f t w.   A
G m t f,   a
    d t w
    w w u t f
    f t w
    w w a t f: a
    i w s.   A
G c t f H.
Addr.____

2.   Ephesians 2:2b; 6:12
according to the prince
of the power of the air [Satan],
the spirit that now worketh ... Ephesians 6:12
For we wrestle not
against flesh and blood, but
against principalities,
against powers,
against the rulers of the darkness
    of this world,
against spiritual wickedness
    in high places.
Eph. 2:2b; 6:12

2.   Ephesians 2:2b; 6:12
a t t p
o t p o t a,
t s t n w ...
F w w n
a f a b, b
a p,
a p,
a t r o t d
  o t w,
a s w
  i h p.
Addr.____

3.   Revelation 12:12b; 2 Cor. 11:3b
Woe to the inhabiters
of the earth   and of the sea!
for the devil
is come down unto you,
having great wrath,
because he knoweth that
he hath but a short time ... 2 Corinthians 11:3b
the serpent [who] beguiled Eve
through his subtilty ...
Rev. 12:12b; 2 Cor. 11:3b

3.   Revelation 12:12b; 2 Cor. 11:3b
W t t i
o t e a o t s!
f t d
i c d u y,
h g w,
b h k t
h h b a s t ...
t s b E
t h s ...
Addr.____

4.   Revelation 12:9b; Ephesians 5:6b
that old serpent,
called the Devil,   and Satan,
which deceiveth the whole world: Ephesians 5:6b
for because of these things
cometh the wrath of God
upon the children of disobedience.
Rev. 12:9b; Eph. 5:6b

4.   Revelation 12:9b; Ephesians 5:6b
t o s,
c t D,   a S,
w d t w w:
f b o t t
c t w o G
u t c o d.
Addr.____

5.   Romans 1:29-32a
Being filled with all unrighteousness,
fornication, wickedness,
covetousness, maliciousness;
full of envy, murder, debate,
deceit, malignity; whisperers,
Backbiters, **haters of God**,
despiteful, proud,
boasters, inventors of evil things,
disobedient to parents,
Without understanding,
covenantbreakers,
without natural affection,
implacable, unmerciful:
Who knowing the judgment of God,   that
they which commit such things
are worthy of death,
Rom. 1:29-32a

5.   Romans 1:29-32a
B f w a u,
f, w,
c, m;
f o e, m, d,
d, m; w,
B, **h o G**,
d, p,
b, i o e t,
d t p,
W u,
c,
w n a,
i, u:
W k t j o G, t
t w c s t
a w o d,
Addr.____

6.   Romans 6:23a
For the wages of sin
is death ...
Rom. 6:23a

6.   Romans 6:23a
F t w o s
i d ...
Addr.____

7.   Romans 3:10,11
As it is written,
There is none   righteous,
no, not one:
There is none   that understandeth,
there is none   that seeketh after God.
Rom. 3:10,11

7.   Romans 3:10,11
A i i w,
T i n r,
n, n o:
T i n t u,
t i n t s a G.
Addr.____

8.   1 John 5:19b
the whole world
lieth in wickedness.
1 Jn. 5:19b

8.   1 John 5:19b
t w w
l i w.
Addr.____

9.   Genesis 3:15
[God said to the serpent] And I will put enmity
between thee   and the woman,   and
between thy seed   and her seed;
it [Jesus] shall bruise thy head,   and
thou [serpent/Satan] shalt bruise **his** heel.
Gen. 3:15

9.   Genesis 3:15
A I w p e
b t   a t w, a
b t s   a h s;
i s b t h,   a
t s b **h** h.
Addr.____

10.   1 John 3:8b
For this purpose
the Son of God   was manifested,   that
he might destroy   the works of the devil.
1 Jn. 3:8b

10.   1 John 3:8b
F t p
t S o G   w m, t
h m d   t w o t d.
Addr.____

11.   John 3:19
And this is the condemnation,   that
light is come into the world,   and
men loved darkness rather than light,
because their deeds were evil.
Jn. 3:19

11.   John 3:19
A t i t c,   t
l i c i t w, a
m l d r t l,
b t d w e.
Addr.____

12.   1 John 2:2
[Jesus] **he** is the propitiation
for our sins: and
not for ours only,   but also
for the sins
of the whole world.
1 Jn. 2:2

12.   1 John 2:2
h i t p
f o s: a
n f o o, b a
f t s
o t w w.
Addr.____

13.   Galatians 3:13
Christ ... being made a curse for us:
for it is written,
Cursed is every one   that
hangeth on a tree:
Gal. 3:13

13.   Galatians 3:13
C ... b m a c f u:
f i i w,
C i e o   t
h o a t:
Addr.____

14.   John 12:32,33
[Jesus said] And I, if I be lifted up
from the earth,
will draw all men unto **me**.
This **he** said, signifying
what death **he** should die.
Jn. 12:32,33

15.   Luke 22:3a,4
Then entered Satan into Judas ... And
he went his way,   and
communed with the chief priests   and
captains, how he might betray
him [Jesus] unto them.
Lk. 22:3a,4

16.   John 12:27
[Jesus said] Now is **my** soul troubled;   and
what shall I say?
Father, save **me** from this hour: but
for this cause came I   unto this hour.
Jn. 12:27

17.   Mark 14:32a,33b,34a-36
And they came to ... Gethsemane: and
[Jesus] **he** began to be sore amazed,   and
to be very heavy ...
My soul is exceeding sorrowful
unto death ...   And
he went forward a little,   and
fell on the ground,   and
prayed   that, if it were possible,
the hour might pass from **him**.   And
he said, Abba, Father,
all things are possible unto **thee**;
take away this cup from **me**:
nevertheless not what I will,   but
what **thou** wilt.
Mk. 14:32a,33b,34a-36

14.   John 12:32,33
A I , i I b l u
f t e ,
w d a m u **m**.
T **h** s, s
w d **h** s d.
Addr.____

15.   Luke 22:3a,4
T e S i J ...   A
h w h w,   a
c w t c p   a
c, h h m b
h u t.
Addr.____

16.   John 12:27
N i **m** s t;   a
w s I s?
F, s **m** f t h: b
f t c c I   u t h.
Addr.____

17.   Mark 14:32a,33b,34a-36
A t c t ... G: a
h b t b s a,   a
t b v h ...
M s i e s
u d ...   A
h w f a l,   a
f o t g,   a
p   t , i i w p,
t h m p f **h**.   A
h s, A, F,
a t a p u **t**;
t a t c f **m**:
n n w I w,   b
w **t** w.
Addr.____

DAY 2:   SAVING FAITH

18.   Mark 14:41b,42b
[Jesus said] the hour is come;
behold, the Son of **man**
is betrayed
into the hands of sinners ...
he [Judas] that betrayeth **me** is at hand.
Mk. 14:41b,42b

18.   Mark 14:41b,42b
t h i c;
b, t S o **m**
i b
i t h o s ...
h t b **m** i a h.
Addr.____

19.   Mark 14:53a,55,56
And they led Jesus away
to the high priest ...   And
the chief priests   and
all the council sought for witness
against Jesus
to put **him** to death;   and
found none.
For many bare false witness
against **him**,   but
their witness agreed not together.
Mk. 14:53a,55,56

19.   Mark 14:53a,55,56
A t l J a
t t h p ...   A
t c p   a
a t c s f w
a J
t p **h** t d;   a
f n.
F m b f w
a **h**,   b
t w a n t.
Addr.____

20.   Luke 22:66,67,70,71
And as soon as it was day,
the elders of the people   and
the chief priests   and
the scribes came together,   and
led **him** into their council, saying,
Art **thou** the Christ?   tell us.   And
he [Jesus] said unto them,
If I tell you,
ye will not believe:
Then said they all,
Art **thou** then the Son of God?   And
he said unto them,
Ye say that I am.   And
they said, What need we
any further witness?
for we ourselves have heard
of **his** own mouth.
Lk. 22:66,67,70,71

20.   Luke 22:66,67,70,71
A a s a i w d,
t e o t p   a
t c p   a
t s c t,   a
l **h** i t c, s,
A t t C? t u. A
h s u t,
I I t y,
y w n b:
T s t a,
A t t t S o G? A
h s u t,
Y s t I a.   A
t s, W n w
a f w?
f w o h h
o **h** o m.
Addr.____

21.   Mark 14:64b,65; 15:1b
And they all condemned **him**
to be guilty of death.   And
some began to spit on **him**,   and
to cover **his** face,   and
to buffet **him**,   and
to say unto **him**, Prophesy: and
the servants did strike **him**
with the palms of their hands.   Mark 15:1b
and bound Jesus,   and
carried **him** away,   and
delivered **him** to Pilate.
Mk. 14:64b,65; 15:1b

21.   Mark 14:64b,65; 15:1b
A t a c **h**
t b g o d.   A
s b t s o **h**,   a
t c **h** f,   a
t b **h**,   a
t s u **h**, P: a
t s d s **h**
w t p o t h.
a b J,   a
c **h** a,   a
d **h** t P.
Addr.____

22.   John 18:37b
Art **thou** a king then? [Pilate asked]
Jesus answered, Thou sayest   that
I am a king.
To this end
was I born,   and
for this cause came I
into the world,   that
I should bear witness
unto the truth.
Jn. 18:37b

22.   John 18:37b
A t a k t?
J a, T s   t
I a a k.
T t e
w I b,   a
f t c c I
i t w,   t
I s b w
u t t.
Addr.____

23.   Mark 15:10,12b-14
... [Pilate] he knew   that
the chief priests
had delivered **him** for envy.
What ... then that I shall do unto **him**
whom ye call
the King of the Jews?   And
they cried out again,
Crucify **him**.
Then Pilate said unto them,
Why, what evil hath **he** done?   And
they cried out the more exceedingly,
Crucify **him**.
Mk. 15:10,12b-14

23.   Mark 15:10,12b-14
... h k   t
t c p
h d **h** f e.
W ... t t I s d u **h**
w y c
t K o t J?   A
t c o a,
C **h**.
T P s u t,
W, w e h **h** d? A
t c o t m e,
C **h**.
Addr.____

24.   Matthew 27:26b-31
when he [Pilate] had scourged Jesus,
he delivered **him**
to be crucified.
Then the soldiers of the governor ...
gathered unto **him**
the whole band of soldiers.   And
they stripped **him**,   and
put on **him** a scarlet robe.   And
when they had platted
a crown of thorns,
they put it upon **his** head,   and
a reed in **his** right hand: and
they bowed the knee before **him**,   and
mocked **him**, saying,
Hail, King of the Jews!   And
they spit upon **him**,   and
took the reed,   and
smote **him**
on the head.   And
after that they had mocked **him**,
they took the robe off from **him**,   and
put **his** own raiment on **him**,   and
led **him** away   to crucify **him**.
Mt. 27:26b-31

24.   Matthew 27:26b-31
w h h s J,
h d **h**
t b c.
T t s o t g ...
g u **h**
t w b o s.   A
t s **h**,   a
p o **h** a s r.   A
w t h p
a c o t,
t p i u **h** h,   a
a r i **h** r h: a
t b t k b **h**,   a
m **h**, s,
H, K o t J!   A
t s u **h**,   a
t t r,   a
s **h**
o t h.   A
a t t h m **h**,
t t t r o f **h**,   a
p **h** o r o **h**, a
l **h** a   t c **h**.
Addr._____

25.   John 19:17
And **he** bearing **his** cross
went forth into a place called
the place of a skull,
which is called
in the Hebrew Golgotha:
Jn. 19:17

25.   John 19:17
A **h** b **h** c
w f i a p c
t p o a s,
w i c
i t H G:
Addr._____

26.   Mark 15:31a,32b
Likewise also the chief priests
mocking ... with the scribes,   And
they that were crucified with **him** [Jesus]
reviled **him**.
Mk. 15:31a,32b

26.   Mark 15:31a,32b
L a t c p
m ... w t s,   A
t t w c w **h**
r **h**.
Addr._____

27.   Luke 23:34,35a
Then said Jesus,
Father, forgive them;
for they know not
what they do.   And
they parted **his** raiment,   and
cast lots.   And
the people stood beholding.
Lk. 23:34,35a

27.   Luke 23:34,35a
T s J,
F, f t;
f t k n
w t d.   A
t p **h** r,   a
c l.   A
t p s b.
Addr.____

28.   Luke 23:44,45a
And it was about the sixth hour,   and
there was a darkness
over all the earth
until the ninth hour.
... the sun was darkened ...
Lk. 23:44,45a

28.   Luke 23:44,45a
A i w a t s h,   a
t w a d
o a t e
u t n h.
... t s w d ...
Addr.____

29.   Matthew 27:46
And about the ninth hour
Jesus cried with a loud voice,
saying, Eli, Eli, lama sabachthani?   that
is to say, My God, **my** God,
why hast **thou** forsaken **me**?
Mt. 27:46

29.   Matthew 27:46
A a t n h
J c w a l v,
s, E, E, l s?   t
i t s, M G, **m** G,
w h t f **m**?
Addr.____

30.   Luke 23:46
And when Jesus had cried
with a loud voice,
he said, Father, into **thy** hands
I commend **my** spirit: and
having said thus,
he gave up the ghost.
Lk. 23:46

30.   Luke 23:46
A w J h c
w a l v,
h s, F, i t h
I c **m** s: a
h s t,
h g u t g.
Addr.____

31.   Mark15:38
And the veil of the temple
was rent in twain
from the top   to the bottom.
Mk.15:38

31.   Mark15:38
A t v o t t
w r i t
f t t t t b.
Addr.____

32.   Genesis 1:8b
And the evening   and the morning
were the second day.
Gen. 1:8b

32.   Genesis 1:8b
A t e   a t m
w t s d.
Addr._____

33.   Romans 10:8,9
But what saith it?   The word is nigh thee,
even in thy mouth,   and
in thy heart: that is,
the word of faith ...   That
if thou shalt confess with   thy mouth
the Lord Jesus,   and
shalt believe in thine heart   that
God hath raised him
from the dead,
thou shalt be saved.
Rom. 10:8,9

33.   Romans 10:8,9
B w s i?   T w i n t,
e i t m,   a
i t h: t i,
t w o f ...   T
i t s c w   t m
t L J,   a
s b i t h   t
G h r h
f t d,
t s b s.
Addr._____

34.   Matthew 12:40
For as Jonas   was three days   and
three nights   in the whale's belly;
so shall the   Son of **man** be three days   and
three nights   in the heart of the earth.
Mt. 12:40

34.   Matthew 12:40
F a J   w t d   a
t n   i t w's b;
s s t   S o m b t d a
t n   i t h o t e.
Addr._____

35.   Romans 10:17
So then faith
cometh by hearing,   and
hearing by the word of God.
Rom. 10:17

35.   Romans 10:17
S t f
c b h, a
h b t w o G.
Addr._____

36.   Hebrews 11:6
But without faith
it is impossible
to please **him**:
for he that cometh to God
must believe that **he** is,   and that
he is a rewarder of them   that
diligently seek **him**.
Heb. 11:6

36.   Hebrews 11:6
B w f
i i i
t p **h**:
f h t c t G
m b t **h** i, a t
h i a r o t t
d s **h**.
Addr._____

DAY THREE: ANALOGY SYNOPSIS

On Creation Day Three,
God's work in Creation was to create dry land called
Earth and the first living organisms – plant life.

This reminds me of the burial of Jesus in the earth. The
third day, He is the firstfruit living – resurrected life.

ANALOGY: CREATION DAY THREE

Analogy: a partial likeness between two things that are compared. This analogy is seeking to view the Scriptures about Jesus and the church through the narrative of Genesis Chapter One.

Creation Day 3: Genesis 1:9-12

9 And God said, Let the waters under the heaven be gathered together unto one place, and let the dry land appear: and it was so. 10 And God called the dry land Earth; and the gathering together of the waters called he Seas: and God saw that it was good. 11 And God said, Let the earth bring forth grass, the herb yielding seed, and the fruit tree yielding fruit after his kind, whose seed is in itself, upon the earth: and it was so. 12 And the earth brought forth grass, and herb yielding seed after his kind, and the tree yielding fruit, whose seed was in itself, after his kind: and God saw that it was good. 13 And the evening and the morning were the third day.

God's Work in Creation: Dry land called Earth, Seas, and vegetation are created on the third day.

Jesus' Work on Earth: Burial and Resurrection: Dry land Earth and vegetation are essential to Jesus' burial. He is buried in the earth, and He is risen on the third day.

Bible Verse Keywords: Dry land Earth; herb; seed; fruit tree; fruit after his kind; whose seed is in itself; myrrh; aloes; linen; spices; bury; garden; sepulchre hewn out in the rock; buried; third day; firstfruits; made alive; resurrection, and the life; shall he live; fruit of his loins; fruit unto holiness; eternal life.

Pondered: 1. The body of Jesus is prepared for burial with a variety of vegetation: a mixture of myrrh (a gum resin from small, spiny trees) and aloes (plant leaves with a bitter juice); and His body is bound with strips of linen (cloth from flax plants) with spices (aromatic substances from plants).

2. The body of Jesus is placed in a new sepulchre hewn out of the rock (the hard part of the earth's crust). The tomb is in a garden (a place of cultivated vegetation). Thus Jesus was laid in a garden, in a tomb, in the Earth.

3. God particularly notes "the fruit tree yielding fruit after his kind, whose seed is in itself." 1 Corinthians 15:20a says, "But now is Christ risen from the dead, and become the firstfruits" of those who died trusting in Him. James 1:18 states, "Of his own will begat he [Jesus Christ] us with the word of truth, that we should be a kind of firstfruits of his creatures."

4. On the third day, the first living organisms of plant life are created. On the third day, the firstfruit living the eternally resurrected life is Jesus.

5. "And God saw that it was good," is declared twice. It is first said for dry land and Seas, and again after the creation of plants – the first earth life.

6. Could be that "good" declared twice brings to mind the Father's joy of: first seeing His Son's body off the cross and buried in the earth, and again after seeing His Son alive – the first resurrected life?

1.   Genesis 1:9,10
And God said,
Let the waters
under the heaven
be gathered together
unto one place,   and
let the dry land appear: and
it was so.   And
God called the dry land Earth;   and
the gathering together of the waters
called **he** Seas: and
God saw that it was good.
Gen. 1:9,10

1.   Genesis 1:9,10
A G s,
L t w
u t h
b g t
u o p,   a
l t d l a: a
i w s.   A
G c t d l E;   a
t g t o t w
c **h** S: a
G s t i w g.
Addr.____

2.   Genesis 1:11
And God said,
Let the earth bring forth grass,
the herb yielding seed,   and
the fruit tree yielding fruit
after his kind,
whose seed is in itself,
upon the earth: and
it was so.
Gen. 1:11

2.   Genesis 1:11
A G s,
L t e b f g,
t h y s,   a
t f t y f
a h k,
w s i i i,
u t e: a
i w s.
Addr.____

3.   John 19:38a-40
... Joseph of Arimathaea ...
took the body of Jesus.   And
there came also Nicodemus ...   and
brought a mixture of
myrrh and aloes,
about an hundred pound weight.
Then took they
the body of Jesus,   and
wound **it** in linen clothes
with the spices,
as the manner of the Jews
is to bury.
Jn. 19:38a-40

3.   John 19:38a-40
... J o A ...
t t b o J.   A
t c a N ...   a
b a m o
m a a,
a a h p w.
T t t
t b o J,   a
w i i l c
w t s,
a t m o t J
i t b.
Addr.____

DAY 3:   STANDING SECURE

ASSURANCE SCRIPTURES

4.   John 19:41,42; Matthew 27:60b
Now in the place
where **he** was crucified
there was a garden;   and
in the garden
a new sepulchre ... Matthew 27:60b
hewn out in the rock ... John 19:41b,42
wherein was never man yet laid.
There laid they Jesus therefore
because of the Jews' preparation day;
for the sepulchre was nigh at hand.
Jn. 19:41,42; Mt. 27:60b

4.   John 19:41,42; Matthew 27:60b
N i t p
w **h** w c
t w a g;   a
i t g
a n s ...
h o i t r ...
w w n m y l.
T l t J t
b o t J' p d;
f t s w n a h.
Addr.____

5.   1 Corinthians 15:1,2a-4
Moreover, brethren,
I declare unto you the gospel
which I preached unto you,
which also ye have received,   and
wherein ye stand;
By which also ye are saved ...   that
Christ died for our sins
according to the scriptures;   And that
he was buried,   and that
he rose again
the third day
according to the scriptures:
1 Cor. 15:1,2a-4

5.   1 Corinthians 15:1,2a-4
M, b,
I d u y t g
w I p u y,
w a y h r,   a
w y s;
B w a y a s ... t
C d f o s
a t t s;   A t
h w b,   a t
h r a
t t d
a t t s:
Addr.____

6.   Matthew 28:1a,5b,6a
In the end of the sabbath,
as it began to dawn toward
the first day of the week ...
the angel ... said unto the women ...
for I know   that
ye seek Jesus,
which was crucified.
He is not here:
for **he** is risen,
as **he** said.
Mt. 28:1a,5b,6a

6.   Matthew 28:1a,5b,6a
I t e o t s,
a i b t d t
t f d o t w ...
t a ... s u t w ...
f I k   t
y s J,
w w c.
H i n h:
f **h** i r,
a **h** s.
Addr.____

7.   Genesis 1:12a
And the earth
brought forth grass,   and
herb yielding seed
after his kind,   and
the tree yielding fruit,
whose seed was in itself,
after his kind:
Gen. 1:12a

7.   Genesis 1:12a
A t e
b f g,   a
h y s
a h k,   a
t t y f,
w s w i i,
a h k:
Addr.____

8.   1 Corinthians 15:20,21
But now is Christ risen
from the dead,   and
become the firstfruits
of them that slept.
For since by man [Adam]
came death,
by **man** [Jesus] came also
the resurrection of the dead.
1 Cor. 15:20,21

8.   1 Corinthians 15:20,21
B n i C r
f t d,   a
b t f
o t t s.
F s b m
c d,
b **m** c a
t r o t d.
Addr.____

9.   1 Corinthians 15:22,23
For as in Adam all die,
even so in Christ
shall all be made alive.   But
every man in his own order:
Christ the firstfruits;
afterward they   that
are Christ's
at **his** coming.
1 Cor. 15:22,23

9.   1 Corinthians 15:22,23
F a i A a d,
e s i C
s a b m a.   B
e m i h o o:
C t f;
a t   t
a C's
a **h** c.
Addr.____

10.   John 11:25
Jesus said ... I am
the resurrection,   and
the life:
he that believeth in **me**,
though he were dead,
yet shall he live:
Jn. 11:25

10.   John 11:25
J s ... I a
t r,   a
t l:
h t b i **m**,
t h w d,
y s h l:
Addr.____

11.   Acts 2:30,31
Therefore being a prophet [King David],   and
knowing   that
God had sworn
with an oath to him,   that
of the fruit of his [King David's] loins,
according to the flesh,
he [God] would raise up Christ
to sit on his [King David's] throne;
He seeing this before spake
of the resurrection
of Christ,   that
his soul was not left in hell,
neither **his** flesh did see corruption.
Acts 2:30,31

11.   Acts 2:30,31
T b a p,   a
k   t
G h s
w a o t h,   t
o t f o h l,
a t t f,
h w r u C
t s o h t;
H s t b s
o t r
o C,   t
h s w n l i h,
n **h** f d s c.
Addr._____

12.   Acts 13:37,38
But **he**,
whom God raised again,
saw no corruption.
Be it known unto you therefore,
men and brethren,   that
through this **man**
is preached unto you
the forgiveness of sins:
Acts 13:37,38

12.   Acts 13:37,38
B **h**,
w G r a,
s n c.
B i k u y t,
m a b,   t
t **t m**
i p u y
t f o s:
Addr._____

13.   Romans 6:22,23
But now
being made free from sin,   and
become servants to God,
ye have your fruit
unto holiness,   and
the end everlasting life.
For the wages of sin
is death;   but
the gift of God
is eternal life
through Jesus Christ our Lord.
Rom. 6:22,23

13.   Romans 6:22,23
B n
b m f f s,   a
b s t G,
y h y f
u h,   a
t e e l.
F t w o s
i d;   b
t g o G
i e l
t J C o L.
Addr._____

14.   Ephesians 2:4b,5a,8,9
God, **who** is rich in mercy,
for **his** great love
wherewith **he** loved us,
Even when we were   dead in sins,
hath quickened us together   with Christ ...
For by grace
are ye saved
through faith ...
it is the gift of God:
Not of works,
lest any man should boast.
Eph. 2:4b,5a,8,9

14.   Ephesians 2:4b,5a,8,9
G, **w** i r i m,
f **h** g l
w **h** l u,
E w w w   d i s,
h q u t   w C ...
F b g
a y s
t f ...
i i t g o G:
N o w,
l a m s b.
Addr.____

15.   1 John 2:1; 1:9
My little children,
these things write I unto you,   that
ye sin not.   And
if any man sin,
we have an **advocate**
with the Father,
Jesus Christ the righteous: 1 John 1:9
If we confess our sins,
he is faithful   and just
to forgive us our sins,   and to cleanse us
from all unrighteousness.
1 Jn. 2:1; 1:9

15.   1 John 2:1; 1:9
M l c,
  t t w I u y, t
y s n.   A
i a m s,
w h a **a**
w t F,
J C t r:
I w c o s,
h i f   a j
t f u o s,   a t c u
f a u.
Addr.____

16.   Psalm 15:1b,2
who shall dwell in **thy** holy hill?
He that walketh uprightly,   and
worketh righteousness,   and
speaketh the truth in his heart.
Ps. 15:1b,2

16.   Psalm 15:1b,2
w s d i t h h?
H t w u,   a
w r,   a
s t t i h h.
Addr.____

17.   Genesis 1:12b,13
and God saw that it was good. And
the evening   and the morning
were the third day.
Gen. 1:12b,13

17.   Genesis 1:12b,13
a G s t i w g. A
t e   a t m
w t t d.
Addr.____

DAY FOUR: ANALOGY SYNOPSIS

On Creation Day Four,
God's work in Creation was to make lights. He made two great lights and the stars also. These created lights bring light to the earth imitating the unique light of Creation Day One.

This reminds me of the prophets and the apostles Jesus commissioned to be His witnesses. These created beings bring light to the earth imitating the True Light, Who returned to His Father.

ANALOGY: CREATION DAY FOUR

Analogy: a partial likeness between two things that are compared. This analogy seeks to view the Scriptures about Jesus and the church through the narrative of Genesis Chapter One.

Creation Day 4: Genesis 1:14-19

14 And God said, Let there be lights in the firmament of the heaven to divide the day from the night; and let them be for signs, and for seasons, and for days, and years: 15 And let them be for lights in the firmament of the heaven to give light upon the earth: and it was so. 16 And God made two great lights; the greater light to rule the day, and the lesser light to rule the night: he made the stars also. 17 And God set them in the firmament of the heaven to give light upon the earth, 18 And to rule over the day and over the night, and to divide the light from the darkness: and God saw that it was good. 19 And the evening and the morning were the fourth day.

God's Work in Creation: God made two great lights, and He made the stars also.

Jesus' Work on Earth: Witnesses: The resurrected Jesus Christ appeared to His apostles. Christ commissioned them to be His witnesses, but they were told to wait for the Holy Spirit. (Pentecost has not come.) Jesus Christ returned to heaven.

Bible Verse Keywords: Lights; day; night; signs; seasons; days; years; true Light; his witnesses; let your light so shine; tarry; received up into heaven; believe in the light; that ye may be the children of light; all the prophets witness; bear witness of the Light; two great lights; greater light to rule the day; lesser light to rule the night; stars; cloud of witnesses; stars of the heavens; not a greater prophet; least of the apostles; sinners, of whom I am chief; less than the least; his witnesses; our conversation is in heaven; to give light on the earth.

Pondered: 1. It is the resurrection of Christ that secures the resurrection of believers. 1 Corinthians 15:13,14 states, "But if there be no resurrection of the dead, then is Christ not risen. And if Christ be not risen, then is our preaching vain, and your faith is also vain." Abraham, King David, all the prophets, and the apostles are some of the "cloud of witnesses" who are sons of His resurrection, sons of the Light, and His lights on earth.

2. God has an order for His church. God states that He appointed to the church – first apostles and second prophets. Of the prophets, Jesus said that John the Baptist was the greatest of all. John came as the testifying witness of the Light, and said that Jesus must increase and I must decrease. Jesus declares that whoever is least in the kingdom of God is greater than John the Baptist. Apostle Paul identifies himself as "less than the least."

3. God first appointed apostles to the church. Of the twelve apostles, it is difficult to think of a more humble and influential apostle than Apostle Paul. He is the "foremost interpreter of Christ through all the ages."MSB NAS

4. Could it be that on Creation Day Four those "made lights" that God set in the firmament are His witnesses on earth – citizens of heaven and His lights on the earth?

DAY 4:   BECOMING CHRISTLIKE

TRANSFORMATION SCRIPTURES

1.   Genesis 1:14
And God said, Let there be lights
in the firmament of the heaven
to divide the day from the night;   and
let them be for signs,   and
for seasons,   and for days,   and years:
Gen. 1:14

1.   Genesis 1:14
A G s, L t b l
i t f o t h
t d t d f t n;   a
l t b f s,   a
f s,   a f d,   a y:
Addr._____

2.   1 Peter 1:20a; John 1:9a; Acts 13:30b
[Jesus] **Who** verily was foreordained
before the foundation of the world,   but
was manifest in these last times ... John 1:9a
That was the true Light ... Acts 13:30b
God raised **him**
from the dead:
1 Pet. 1:20a; Jn. 1:9a; Acts 13:30b

2.   1 Pet. 1:20a; John 1:9a; Acts 13:30b
W v w f
b t f o t w,   b
w m i t l t ...
T w t t L ...
 G r **h**
f t d:
Addr._____

3.   Acts 1:3b
[Jesus] **he** shewed **himself** alive
after **his** passion
by many infallible proofs,
being seen of them forty days,   and
speaking of the things
pertaining to the kingdom of God:
Acts 1:3b

3.   Acts 1:3b
h s **h** a
a **h** p
b m i p,
b s o t f d,   a
s o t t
p t t k o G:
Addr._____

4.   Acts 13:31
And **he** was seen many days
of them which came up with **him**
from Galilee to Jerusalem,
who are **his** witnesses
unto the people.
Acts 13:31

4.   Acts 13:31
A **h** w s m d
o t w c u w **h**
f G t J,
w a **h** w
u t p.
Addr._____

5.   Luke 24:36b
Jesus **himself** stood
in the midst of them,   and
saith unto them,
Peace be unto you.
Lk. 24:36b

5.   Luke 24:36b
J **h** s
i t m o t,   a
s u t,
P b u y.
Addr._____

6. Luke 24:39,45	6. Luke 24:39,45
[Jesus said] Behold **my** hands and	B **m** h a
my feet, that	**m** f, t
it is I **myself**:	i i I **m**:
handle **me**, and see;	h **m**, a s;
for a spirit hath not	f a s h n
flesh and bones,	f a b,
as ye see **me** have.	a y s **m** h.
Then opened **he**	T o **h**
their understanding, that	t u, t
they might understand	t m u
the scriptures,	t s,
Lk. 24:39,45	Addr.____

7. John 15:27	7. John 15:27
And ye [apostles] also	A y a
shall bear witness,	s b w,
because ye have been with **me**	b y h b w **m**
from the beginning.	f t b.
Jn. 15:27	Addr.____

8. Matthew 5:16	8. Matthew 5:16
Let your light so shine	L y l s s
before men, that	b m, t
they may see your good works, and	t m s y g w, a
glorify your Father	g y F
which is in heaven.	w i i h.
Mt. 5:16	Addr.____

9. Luke 24:49b; Mark 16:19	9. Luke 24:49b; Mark 16:19
[Jesus said] but tarry ye in ... Jerusalem,	b t y i ... J,
until ye be endued	u y b e
with power from on high. Mark 16:19	w p f o h.
So then after the Lord	S t a t L
had spoken unto them,	h s u t,
he was received up	**h** w r u
into heaven, and	i h, a
sat on the right hand of God.	s o t r h o G.
Lk. 24:49b; Mk. 16:19	Addr.____

10.   Genesis 1:15
[God said] And let them be for lights
in the firmament of the heaven
to give light upon the earth: and it was so.
Gen. 1:15

10.   Genesis 1:15
A l t b f l
i t f o t h
t g l u t e: a i w s.
Addr.____

11.   John 12:36a
While ye have light,
believe in the light [Jesus],   that
ye may be the children of light.
Jn. 12:36a

11.   John 12:36a
W y h l,
b i t l,   t
y m b t c o l.
Addr.____

12.   Ecclesiastes 3:1
To every thing   there is a season,   and
a time to every   purpose under the heaven:
Eccl. 3:1

12.   Ecclesiastes 3:1
T e t   t i a s,   a
a t t e   p u t h:
Addr.____

13.   1 Peter 1:20a; Acts 10:43
[Jesus] **Who** verily was foreordained
before the foundation of the world ... Acts 10:43
To **him** give all the prophets witness,   that
through **his** name
whosoever believeth in **him**
shall receive remission of sins.
1 Pet. 1:20a; Acts 10:43

13.   1 Peter 1:20a; Acts 10:43
W v w f
b t f o t w ...
T **h** g a t p w,   t
t **h** n
w b i **h**
s r r o s.
Addr.____

14.   Hebrews 12:1b; Isaiah 61:1,2a
we also are compassed about with
so great a cloud of witnesses ... Isaiah 61:1,2a
[Isaiah prophesied Jesus]   The Spirit of
the Lord GOD   is upon **me**;
because the LORD   hath anointed **me**
to preach good tidings   unto the meek;
he hath sent **me**   to bind up the brokenhearted,
to proclaim liberty   to the captives, and
the opening of the prison   to them   that
are bound;
To proclaim the acceptable year
of the LORD,
Heb. 12:1b; Is. 61:1,2a

14.   Hebrews 12:1b; Isaiah 61:1,2a
w a a c a w
s g a c o w ...
T S o
t L G   i u **m**;
b t L   h a **m**
t p g t   u t m;
h h s **m**   t b u t b,
t p l   t t c,   a
t o o t p   t t   t
a b;
T p t a y
o t L,
Addr.____

15. John 1:23,7,8; 3:30; Daniel 4:3a
[John the Baptist declared] He said, I am
the voice of one crying in the wilderness,
Make straight the way of the Lord,
as said the prophet Esaias. John 1:7,8
The same came for a witness,
to bear witness of the Light [Jesus], that
all men through him might believe.
He was not that Light, but
was sent to bear witness of that Light. John 3:30
He [Jesus] must increase, but
I [John] must decrease. Dan. 4:3a
How great are **his** signs!
Jn. 1:23,7,8; 3:30; Dan. 4:3a

15. John 1:23,7,8; 3:30; Daniel 4:3a
H s, I a
t v o o c i t w,
M s t w o t L,
a s t p E.
T s c f a w,
t b w o t L, t
a m t h m b.
H w n t L, b
w s t b w o t L.
H m i, b
I m d.
H g a **h** s!
Addr.____

16. Genesis 1:16
And God made two great lights;
the greater light to rule the day, and
the lesser light to rule the night:
he made the stars also.
Gen. 1:16

16. Genesis 1:16
A G m t g l;
t g l t r t d, a
t l l t r t n:
h m t s a.
Addr.____

17. Hebrews 12:1b; Genesis 26:4
... so great a cloud of witnesses ... Genesis 26:4
[God said to Abraham] ... I will make
thy seed to multiply
as the stars of heaven, and
will give unto thy seed
all these countries; and
in thy seed shall all the nations
of the earth be blessed;
Heb. 12:1b; Gen. 26:4

17. Hebrews 12:1b; Genesis 26:4
... s g a c o w ...
... I w m
t s t m
a t s o h, a
w g u t s
a t c; a
i t s s a t n
o t e b b;
Addr.____

18. Galatians 3:16
Now to Abraham and his seed
were the promises made.
[God] He saith not, And to seeds,
as of many; but as of one,
And to thy seed, **which** is Christ.
Gal. 3:16

18. Galatians 3:16
N t A a h s
w t p m.
H s n, A t s,
a o m; b a o o,
A t t s, **w** i C.
Addr.____

19.   1 Corinthians 12:28a
And God hath set some   in the church,

first apostles,
secondarily prophets ...
1 Cor. 12:28a

19.   1 Corinthians 12:28a
A G h s s   i t c,

f a,
s p ...
Addr.____

20.   Luke 7:28
[Jesus said] For I say unto you,
Among those   that
are born of women
there is not a greater prophet
than John the Baptist: but

he that is least
in the kingdom of God
is greater than he.
Lk. 7:28

20.   Luke 7:28
F I s u y,
A t   t
a b o w
t i n a g p
t J t B: b

h t i l
i t k o G
i g t h.
Addr.____

21.   1 Corinthians 15:9,10a
[Paul said] For I am

the least of the apostles,
that am not meet
to be called an apostle,
because I persecuted
the church of God. But
by the grace of God
I am what I am: and
his grace which was
bestowed upon me
was not in vain;
1 Cor. 15:9,10a

21.   1 Corinthians 15:9,10a
F I a

t l o t a,
t a n m
t b c a a,
b I p
t c o G.   B
b t g o G
I a w I a: a
h g w w
b u m
w n i v;
Addr.____

22.   1 Timothy 1:15b
[Paul said] Christ Jesus came into the world
to save sinners;

of whom I am chief.
1 Tim. 1:15b

22.   1 Timothy 1:15b
C J c i t w
t s s;

o w I a c.
Addr.____

23.   Ephesians 3:8
[Paul said] Unto me, who am

less than the least of all saints,
is this grace given,   that
I should preach
among the Gentiles
the unsearchable riches of Christ;
Eph. 3:8

24.   Acts 10:42
And [Jesus] **he** commanded us [apostles]
to preach unto the people,   and
to testify   that
it is **he**
which was ordained of God
to be the Judge of quick   and
dead.
Acts 10:42

25.   Acts 5:32b; Philippians 3:20
we are **his** witnesses of these things; Phil. 3:20
For our conversation is in heaven;
from whence also we look for
the Saviour, the Lord Jesus Christ:
Acts 5:32b; Phil. 3:20

26.   Genesis 1:17-19
And God set them
in the firmament of the heaven
to give light upon the earth,   And
to rule over the day   and
over the night,   and
to divide the light
from the darkness: and

God saw that it was good.   And
the evening and the morning
were the fourth day.
Gen. 1:17-19

---

23.   Ephesians 3:8
U m, w a

l t t l o a s,
i t g g,   t
I s p
a t G
t u r o C;
Addr._____

24.   Acts 10:42
A **h** c u
t p u t p,   a
t t   t
i i **h**
w w o o G
t b t J o q   a
d.
Addr._____

25.   Acts 5:32b; Philippians 3:20
w a **h** w o t t;
F o c i i h;
f w a w l f
t S, t L J C:
Addr._____

26.   Genesis 1:17-19
A G s t
i t f o t h
t g l u t e,   A
t r o t d   a
o t n,   a
t d t l
f t d: a

G s t i w g.   A
t e a t m
w t f d.
Addr._____

DAY FIVE: ANALOGY SYNOPSIS

On Creation Day Five,
God's work in Creation was to create a new
kind of life – flesh and blood water creatures,
generally called fish, and afterwards birds that
fly above the earth.

This reminds me of Christ creating a new life
in the flesh and blood apostles – fishers of men,
and afterwards recipients of the Holy Spirit, Who
often is symbolically represented as a dove
flying above the earth.

ANALOGY: CREATION DAY FIVE

Analogy: a partial likeness between two things that are compared. This analogy seeks to view the Scriptures about Jesus and the church through the narrative of Genesis Chapter One.

Creation Day 5: Genesis 1:20-23

20 And God said, Let the waters bring forth abundantly the moving creature that hath life, and fowl that may fly above the earth in the open firmament of heaven. 21 And God created great whales, and every living creature that moveth, which the waters brought forth abundantly, after their kind, and every winged fowl after his kind: and God saw that it was good. 22 And God blessed them, saying, Be fruitful, and multiply, and fill the waters in the seas, and let fowl multiply in the earth. 23 And the evening and the morning were the fifth day.

God's Work in Creation: Water creatures, generally called fish, and then birds are created.

Jesus' Work on Earth: Great Commission and Pentecost: The apostles submitting to the new command to love others, are in one accord. Thereby the Holy Spirit comes.

Bible Verse Keywords: Waters bring forth abundantly the moving creatures; fowl that may fly above; new commandment; love one another; I have loved you; new creature; make you become fishers of men; the Holy Ghost descended ... like a dove; except a man be born of water and of the Spirit; It is the spirit that quickeneth; the flesh profiteth nothing; Go ... teach all nations; filled with the Holy Ghost; Lord added to the church daily; greater is he that is in you; love God; he who loveth God love his brother also; leaving us an example; we are ambassadors for Christ; ministry of reconciliation.

Pondered: 1. All kinds of sea creatures, generally called fish, are created and live in peace. Commissioned by Jesus as fishers of men and living out the new love commandment, the disciples live in peace awaiting the Holy Spirit.

2. God created birds. The dove is often symbolic of the Holy Spirit. At Pentecost the Holy Spirit comes to indwell the disciples with power.

3. On Day Five, God created new living creations – unlike plant life. These are flesh and blood water creatures, and afterwards birds. Jesus gave a new life to the flesh and blood apostles. They were born again, baptized, and afterwards filled with the Holy Spirit. Christ created new living creations of spiritual life – unlike natural life.

4. Some of the water creatures are mammals; their offspring will be born. Thus waters brought forth abundantly fish. After Pentecost Peter, a fisher of men, preaches the gospel and thousands from every nation are born again. Thus waters brought forth abundantly believers being baptized.

5. Could it be that God's sequence of creating fish, and afterwards birds, mirrors the sequence of commissioning the fishers of men, and afterwards giving them the Holy Spirit (often depicted as a dove)?

DAY 5:   GLORIFYING GOD

1.   Genesis 1:20
And God said, Let the waters
bring forth abundantly
the moving creature   that hath life,   and

fowl that may fly above the earth
in the open firmament of heaven.
Gen. 1:20

2.   John 13:34a,35a
[Jesus said] A new commandment
I give unto you,   That
ye love one another;
as I have loved you ...
By this
shall all men know   that
ye are **my** disciples,
Jn. 13:34a,35a

3.   2 Corinthians 5:17; Mark 1:17
Therefore if any man be in Christ,
he is a new creature:
old things are passed away;
behold, all things are become new. Mark 1:17
... Jesus said unto them,
Come ye after **me**, and
I will make you
become fishers of men.
2 Cor. 5:17; Mk. 1:17

4.   1 John 5:6
This is **he** [Jesus] that came
by water and blood,
even Jesus Christ;
not by water only,   but
by water and blood.   And
it is the Spirit   that
beareth witness,
because the Spirit is truth.
1 Jn. 5:6

MATURATION SCRIPTURES

1.   Genesis 1:20
A G s, L t w
b f a
t m c   t h l, a

f t m f a t e
i t o f o h.
Addr._____

2.   John 13:34a,35a
A n c
I g u y,   T
y l o a;
a I h l y ...
B t
s a m k   t
y a **m** d,
Addr._____

3.   2 Corinthians 5:17; Mark 1:17
T i a m b i C,
h i a n c:
o t a p a;
b, a t a b n.
... J s u t,
C y a **m**, a
I w m y
b f o m.
Addr._____

4.   1 John 5:6
T i **h** t c
b w a b,
e J C;
n b w o, b
b w a b. A
i i t S   t
b w,
b t S i t.
Addr._____

5.   Luke 3:21b,22
Jesus also being baptized,   And
the Holy Ghost [had] descended

in a bodily shape   like a dove upon **him**, and
a **voice**   came from heaven,
which said,   **Thou** art **my** beloved Son;
in **thee**   I am well pleased.
Lk. 3:21b,22

6.   John 3:5b; 1 John 5:1a
[Jesus said] Except a man be born
of water and of the Spirit,
he cannot enter into
the kingdom of God. 1 John 5:1a
Whosoever believeth   that
Jesus is the Christ
is born of God:
Jn. 3:5b; 1 Jn. 5:1a

7.   John 3:3,5b
Jesus ... said ... Verily, verily,
I say unto thee,
Except a man be born again,
he cannot see
the kingdom of God.
Except a man be born of water   and
of the Spirit,
he cannot enter
into the kingdom of God.
Jn. 3:3,5b

8.   John 6:63
It is the **spirit**   that quickeneth;
the flesh profiteth
nothing:
the words that I speak unto you,
they are spirit,   and
they are life.
Jn. 6:63

5.   Luke 3:21b,22
J a b b,   A
t H G d

i a b s   l a d u **h**, a
a **v**   c f h,
w s,   **T** a **m** b S;
i **t**   I a w p.
Addr._____

6.   John 3:5b; 1 John 5:1a
E a m b b
o w a o t S,
h c e i
t k o G.
W b   t
J i t C
i b o G:
Addr._____

7.   John 3:3,5b
J ... s ... V, v,
I s u t,
E a m b b a,
h c s
t k o G.
E a m b b o w   a
o t S,
h c e
i t k o G.
Addr._____

8.   John 6:63
I i t **s**   t q;
t f p
n:
t w t I s u y,
t a s,   a
t a l.
Addr._____

9.   Mark 16:15; Matthew 28:18b,19
And [Jesus] **he** said unto them,
Go ye into all the world, and
preach the gospel
to every creature. Matthew 28:18b,19
All power is given   unto **me**
in heaven and in earth.
Go ye therefore,   and
teach all nations,
baptizing them in the name
of the Father,   and
of the Son,   and
of the Holy Ghost:
Mk. 16:15; Mt. 28:18b,19

9.   Mark 16:15; Matthew 28:18b,19
A **h** s u t,
G y i a t w, a
p t g
t e c.
A p i g   u **m**
i h a i e.
G y t,   a
t a n,
b t i t n
o t F,   a
o t S,   a
o t H G:
Addr.____

10.   Acts 1:4a,5
And, being assembled together with them,
[Jesus] commanded them   that
they should not depart   from Jerusalem, but
wait for the promise of the Father ...
For John truly baptized   with water;   but
ye shall be baptized   with the Holy Ghost
not many days hence.
Acts 1:4a,5

10.   Acts 1:4a,5
A, b a t w t,
c t   t
t s n d   f J,   b
w f t p o t F ...
F J t b   w w; b
y s b b   w t H G
n m d h.
Addr.____

11.   Acts 2:1a,2a,4; 4:31b
And when the day of Pentecost
was fully come,
they were all with one accord ... And
suddenly there came
a sound from heaven
as of a rushing mighty wind,   And
they were all filled
with the Holy Ghost,   and
began to speak with other tongues,
as the Spirit gave them utterance. Acts 4:31b
and they spake
the word of God
with boldness.
Acts 2:1a,2a,4; 4:31b

11.   Acts 2:1a,2a,4; 4:31b
A w t d o P
w f c,
t w a w o a ... A
s t c
a s f h
a o a r m w, A
t w a f
w t H G,   a
b t s w o t,
a t S g t u.
a t s
t w o G
w b.
Addr.____

12.   Acts 2:38
... Peter said unto them [the multitude from every nation],
Repent,   and
be baptized   every one of you
in the name of Jesus Christ
for the remission of sins,   and
ye shall receive
the gift
of the Holy Ghost.
Acts 2:38

13.   Acts 2:41,47b
Then they   that gladly received
his word   were baptized: and
the same day there were added unto them
about three thousand souls.   And
the Lord added to the church daily
such as should be saved.
Acts 2:41,47b

14.   1 John 4:4
Ye are of God, little children,   and
have overcome them:
because greater is **he**   that
is in you,
than he that is in the world.
1 Jn. 4:4

15.   1 Corinthians 2:9,10
But as it is written,
Eye hath not seen,   nor ear heard,
neither have entered   into the heart of man,
the things which God hath prepared
for them that love **him**.   But
God hath revealed them unto us
by **his** Spirit:
for the Spirit searcheth
all things,
yea, the deep things of God.
1 Cor. 2:9,10

12.   Acts 2:38
... P s u t,
R,   a
b b e o o y
i t n o J C
f t r o s, a
y s r
t g
o t H G.
Addr.____

13.   Acts 2:41,47b
T t   t g r
h w   w b: a
t s d t w a u t
a t t s.   A
t L a t t c d
s a s b s.
Addr.____

14.   1 John 4:4
Y a o G, l c, a
h o t:
b g i **h**   t
i i y,
t h t i i t w.
Addr.____

15.   1 Corinthians 2:9,10
B a i i w,
E h n s, n e h,
n h e   i t h o m,
t t w G h p
f t t l **h**. B
G h r t u u
b **h** S:
f t S s
a t,
y, t d t o G.
Addr.____

16.   1 John 4:20,21; 2:5
If a man say, I love God,   and
hateth his brother,
he is a liar:
for he that loveth not his brother
whom he hath seen,
how can he love God
whom he hath not seen?   And
this commandment
have we from **him**,   That
he who loveth God
love his brother also.
But whoso keepeth **his** word,
in him verily
is the love of God
perfected:
hereby know we   that
we are in **him**.
1 Jn. 4:20,21; 2:5

16.   1 John 4:20,21; 2:5
I a m s, I l G,   a
h h b,
h i a l:
f h t l n h b
w h h s,
h c h l G
w h h n s?   A
t c
h w f **h**,   T
h w l G
l h b a.
B w k **h** w,
i h v
i t l o G
p:
h k w   t
w a i **h**.
Addr._____

17.   1 Peter 2:23
[Christ] **Who**, when **he** was reviled,
reviled not again;
when **he** suffered,
he threatened not;   but
committed **himself**
to **him** [Father God]   that
judgeth righteously:
1 Pet. 2:23

17.   1 Peter 2:23
W, w **h** w r,
r n a;
w **h** s,
h t n; b
c **h**
t **h**   t
j r:
Addr.____

18.   1 Peter 2:21,22
For even hereunto
were ye called: because
Christ also suffered for us,
leaving us an example,   that
ye should follow **his** steps:
Who did no sin,
neither was guile found
in **his** mouth:
1 Pet. 2:21,22

18.   1 Peter 2:21,22
F e h
w y c: b
C a s f u,
l u a e, t
y s f **h** s:
W d n s,
n w g f
i **h** m:
Addr.____

DAY 5:   GLORIFYING GOD

19.   2 Corinthians 5:20
Now then
we are ambassadors
for Christ,
as though God
did beseech you
by us:
we pray you
in Christ's stead,
be ye reconciled to God.
2 Cor. 5:20

20.   2 Corinthians 5:18
And all things are of God,
who hath reconciled us
to **himself**
by Jesus Christ,   and
hath given to us
the ministry of reconciliation;
2 Cor. 5:18

21.   Romans 12:14,16,17a,19
Bless them which persecute you:
bless, and curse not.
Be of the same mind
one toward another.
Mind not high things,   but
condescend to men
of low estate.
Be not wise
in your own conceits.
Recompense to no man
evil for evil.
Dearly beloved,
avenge not yourselves,   but
rather give place unto wrath: for
it is written,
Vengeance is **mine**;
I will repay, saith the Lord.
Rom. 12:14,16,17a,19

MATURATION SCRIPTURES

19.   2 Corinthians 5:20
N t
w a a
f C,
a t G
d b y
b u:
w p y
i C's s,
b y r t G.
Addr._____

20.   2 Corinthians 5:18
A a t a o G,
w h r u
t **h**
b J C,   a
h g t u
t m o r;
Addr._____

21.   Romans 12:14,16,17a,19
B t w p y:
b, a c n.
B o t s m
o t a.
M n h t,   b
c t m
o l e.
B n w
i y o c.
R t n m
e f e.
D b,
a n y,   b
r g p u w: f
i i w,
V i **m**;
I w r, s t L.
Addr._____

22.   Romans 12:20a
Therefore [saith the Lord]
if thine enemy hunger,
feed him;
if he thirst,
give him drink:
Rom. 12:20a

23.   Matthew 7:14b
strait is the gate,   and
narrow is the way,
which leadeth unto life,   and
few there be   that
find it.
Mt. 7:14b

24.   Genesis 1:21
And God created
great whales,   and
every living creature   that moveth,
which the waters
brought forth abundantly,
after their kind,   and
every winged fowl
after his kind: and
God saw that it was good.
Gen. 1:21

25.   Genesis 1:22,23
And God blessed them,
saying,
Be fruitful,   and
multiply, and fill
the waters in the seas,   and
let fowl multiply
in the earth.
And the evening   and
the morning
were the fifth day.
Gen. 1:22,23

22.   Romans 12:20a
T
i t e h,
f h;
i h t,
g h d:
Addr._____

23.   Matthew 7:14b
s i t g,   a
n i t w,
w l u l,   a
f t b   t
f i.
Addr._____

24.   Genesis 1:21
A G c
g w,   a
e l c   t m,
w t w
b f a,
a t k,   a
e w f
a h k: a
G s t i w g.
Addr._____

25.   Genesis 1:22,23
A G b t,
s,
B f,   a
m, a f
t w i t s, a
l f m
i t e.
A t e   a
t m
w t f d.
Addr._____

DAY SIX: ANALOGY SYNOPSIS

On Creation Day Six,
God's work in Creation was to create land animals –
cattle for domesticated animals, beast for wild animals,
and "creeping thing." In His image, God created
man – male and female. God presents to Adam, Eve,
his bride.

This reminds me of Christ creating His bride – the church
of sheep from every nation; but beforehand as the Lord
forewarned, deceiving wolves and "that old serpent"
will stir up self-worship among the sheep. Faithful sheep,
living out the two greatest commandments – of trusting
unreservedly in the Lord, and secondly, sharing His
reconciling love – will be ready when the Bridegroom
comes – Rev. 3:7-13. Jesus Christ will present to Himself
His bride.

ANALOGY: CREATION DAY SIX

Analogy: a partial likeness between two things that are compared. This analogy seeks to view the Scriptures about Jesus and the church through the narrative of Genesis Chapter One.

Creation Day 6: Genesis 1:24-31

24 And God said, Let the earth bring forth the living creature after his kind, cattle, and creeping thing, and beast of the earth after his kind: and it was so. 25 And God made the beast of the earth after his kind, and cattle after their kind, and every thing that creepeth upon the earth after his kind: and God saw that it was good. 26 And God said, Let us make man in our image, after our likeness: and let them have dominion over the fish of the sea, and over the fowl of the air, and over the cattle, and over all the earth, and over every creeping thing that creepeth upon the earth. 27 So God created man in his own image, in the image of God created he him; male and female created he them. 28 And God blessed them, and God said unto them, Be fruitful, and multiply, and replenish the earth, and subdue it: and have dominion over the fish of the sea, and over the fowl of the air, and over every living thing that moveth upon the earth. 29 And God said, Behold, I have given you every herb bearing seed, which is upon the face of all the earth, and every tree, in the which is the fruit of a tree yielding seed; to you it shall be for meat. 30 And to every beast of the earth, and to every fowl of the air, and to every thing that creepeth upon the earth, wherein there is life, I have given every green herb for meat: and it was so. 31 And God saw every thing that he had made, and, behold, it was very good. And the evening and the morning were the sixth day.

God's Work in Creation: God created land animals: domesticated and wild animals, and creeping things. In His own image, God created man – male and female.

Jesus' Work on Earth: Marriage: The church is awaiting her Bridegroom. Jesus forewarned about false prophets and false teachers deceiving many in the last days.

Bible Verse Keywords: Cattle; creeping thing; beast; sheep in the midst of wolves; false prophets ... in sheep's clothing; ravening wolves; the abundance of his heart; by thy words; mercy rejoiceth against judgement; why call ye me, Lord, Lord; beware ye of the leaven of the Pharisees; the good shepherd; giveth his life for the sheep; God created man in his own image; male and female; the two shall become one flesh; concerning Christ; cherisheth; as the Lord does the church; married to ... him; Christ also loved the church; gave himself for it; certain king which made a marriage.

Pondered: 1. Land animals such as sheep, wolves, and serpent are created. Jesus said that in the last days, Satan, "that serpent of old," will deceive many, and so will wolves masquerading as sheep. Ever since the beautiful and anointed angel, Lucifer, later called Satan, measured and compared his self as best, one's eternity concludes on Christ's Lordship or fatal self-worship. True Christ-followers reject the satanic spirit of exalting self which poisoned a third of the holy angels, all earth, and for a time the Early Church.

2. Adam and Eve, Christ and His bride – each one flesh.

3. Could it be that some land animals bring to mind how Satan and false teachers deceive, while Adam and Eve are a typology of the Lord Jesus Christ marrying His bride – the church of sheep from every nation?

1.   Genesis 1:24
And God said,
Let the earth bring forth
the living creature after his kind,
cattle,   and
creeping thing,   and
beast of the earth
after his kind: and
it was so.
Gen. 1:24

1.   Genesis 1:24
A G s,
L t e b f
t l c a h k,
c,   a
c t,   a
b o t e
a h k: a
i w s.
Addr.____

2.   Matthew 10:16; 7:15,16a
Behold, I send you forth
as sheep
in the midst of wolves:
be ye therefore wise as serpents,   and
harmless as doves.
Beware of false prophets,
which come to you   in sheep's clothing,   but
inwardly they are   ravening wolves.
Ye shall know them by their fruits.
Mt. 10:16; 7:15,16a

2.   Matthew 10:16; 7:15,16a
B, I s y f
a s
i t m o w:
b y t w a s,   a
h a d.
B o f p,
w c t y   i s's c,   b
i t a   r w.
Y s k t   b t f.
Addr.____

3.   Luke 6:44a,45b; Matthew 12:36,37
For every tree is known
by his own fruit.
for of the abundance
of the heart
his mouth speaketh. Matthew 12:36,37

3.   Luke 6:44a,45b; Matthew 12:36,37
F e t i k
b h o f.
f o t a
o t h
h m s.

But I say unto you,   That
every idle word   that
men shall speak,
they shall give account thereof
in the day of judgment.
For by thy words
thou shalt be justified, and
by thy words
thou shalt be condemned.
Lk. 6:44a,45b; Mt. 12:36,37

B I s u y,   T
e i w   t
m s s,
t s g a t
i t d o j.
F b t w
t s b j,   a
b t w
t s b c.
Addr.____

4.   Hebrews 13:15,16
By **him** therefore
let us offer the sacrifice
of praise to God continually,   that is,
the fruit of our lips
giving thanks to **his** name.   But
to do good   and
to communicate forget not:
for with such sacrifices
God is well pleased.
Heb. 13:15,16

4.   Hebrews 13:15,16
B **h** t
l u o t s
o p t G c,   t i,
t f o o l
g t t **h** n.   B
t d g   a
t c f n:
f w s s
G i w p.
Addr._____

5.   Matthew 25:31,33-37a,40
When the Son of man shall come
in **his** glory ...
then shall **he** sit upon
the throne of **his** glory: And
he shall set the sheep
on **his** right hand,   but
the goats on the left.
Then shall the King say
unto them on **his** right hand,
Come, ye blessed of **my** Father,
inherit the kingdom prepared for you
from the foundation of the world:
For I was an hungred,   and ye gave **me** meat:
I was thirsty,   and ye gave **me** drink:
I was a stranger,   and ye took **me** in:
Naked,   and ye clothed **me**:
I was sick,   and ye visited **me**:
I was in prison,   and ye came unto **me**.
Then shall the righteous answer **him**, saying,
Lord, when saw we **thee** ... And
the King shall answer   and
say unto them,
Verily I say unto you, Inasmuch as
ye have done it unto one
of the least of these **my** brethren,
ye have done it unto **me**.
Mt. 25:31,33-37a,40

5.   Matthew 25:31,33-37a,40
W t S o m s c
i **h** g ...
t s **h** s u
t t o **h** g: A
h s s t s
o **h** r h,   b
t g o t l.
T s t K s
u t o **h** r h,
C, y b o **m** F,
i t k p f y
f t f o t w:
F I w a h,   a y g **m** m:
I w t,   a y g **m** d:
I w a s,   a y t **m** i:
N,   a y c **m**:
I w s,   a y v **m**:
I w i p,   a y c u **m**.
T s t r a **h**, s,
L, w s w t ...   A
t K s a   a
s u t,
V I s u y, I a
y h d i u o
o t l o t **m** b,
y h d i u **m**.
Addr._____

6.   James 2:13; Luke 6:36,46
For he shall have judgment
without mercy,   that
hath shewed no mercy;   and
mercy rejoiceth against judgment. Luke 6:36,46
Be ye therefore merciful,
as your Father also is merciful. And
why call ye **me**,
Lord, Lord,   and
do not the things which I say?
Js. 2:13; Lk. 6:36,46

6.   James 2:13; Luke 6:36,46
F h s h j
w m,   t
h s n m;   a
m r a j.
B y t m,
a y F a i m. A
w c y **m**,
L, L,   a
d n t t w I s?
Addr.____

7.   Luke 12:1b-3
he began to say unto **his** disciples
first of all,
Beware ye of the leaven of the Pharisees,
which is hypocrisy.
For there is nothing covered,   that
shall not be revealed;
neither hid,   that shall not be known.
Therefore whatsoever
ye have spoken in darkness
shall be heard in the light;   and that
which ye have spoken in the ear in closets
shall be proclaimed upon the housetops.
Lk. 12:1b-3

7.   Luke 12:1b-3
h b t s u **h** d
f o a,
B y o t l o t P,
w i h.
F t i n c,   t
s n b r;
n h,   t s n b k.
T w
y h s i d
s b h i t l;   a t
w y h s i t e i c
s b p u t h.
Addr.____

8.   Matthew 7:12,13
Therefore all things
whatsoever ye would   that
men should do to you,
do ye even so to them:
for this is the law   and the prophets.
Enter ye in at the strait gate:
for wide is the gate,   and
broad is the way,   that
leadeth to destruction, and
many there be
which go in thereat:
Mt. 7:12,13

8.   Matthew 7:12,13
T a t
w y w   t
m s d t y,
d y e s t t:
f t i t l   a t p.
E y i a t s g:
f w i t g,   a
b i t w,   t
l t d,   a
m t b
w g i t:
Addr.____

9.   John 10:7b,11,14b,15b
Verily, verily, I say unto you,
I am the door of the sheep.
I am the good shepherd:
the good shepherd
giveth **his** life   for the sheep.
I ... know **my** sheep,   and
am known of **mine**.
I lay down **my** life   for the sheep.
Jn. 10:7b,11,14b,15b

10.   Matthew 7:14b
strait is the gate,   and
narrow is the way,
which leadeth unto life,   and
few there be   that
find it.
Mt. 7:14b

11.   Genesis 1:25
And God made the beast of the earth
after his kind,   and
cattle after their kind,   and
every thing that creepeth upon the earth
after his kind: and
God saw that it was good.
Gen. 1:25

12.   Genesis 1:26
And God said,
Let **us** make man in **our** image,
after **our** likeness: and
let them have dominion
over the fish of the sea,   and
over the fowl of the air,   and
over the cattle,   and
over all the earth,   and
over every creeping thing   that
creepeth upon the earth.
Gen. 1:26

9.   John 10:7b,11,14b,15b
V, v, I s u y,
I a t d o t s.
I a t g s:
t g s
g **h** l   f t s.
I ... k **m** s,   a
a k o **m**.
I l d **m** l   f t s.
Addr._____

10.   Matthew 7:14b
s i t g,   a
n i t w,
w l u l,   a
f t b   t
f i.
Addr._____

11.   Genesis 1:25
A G m t b o t e
a h k,   a
c a t k,   a
e t t c u t e
a h k: a
G s t i w g.
Addr._____

12.   Genesis 1:26
A G s,
L **u** m m i **o** i,
a **o** l: a
l t h d
o t f o t s,   a
o t f o t a,   a
o t c,   a
o a t e,   a
o e c t   t
c u t e.
Addr._____

13.   Genesis 1:27; 2:24
So God created man   in **his** own image,
in the image of God   created **he** him;
male and female created   **he** them. Genesis 2:24
Therefore shall man leave
his father and his mother, and
cleave unto his wife: and
they shall be one flesh.
Gen. 1:27; 2:24

14.   Ephesians 5:31,32
For this cause shall a man leave
his father and mother,   and
shall be joined unto his wife,   and
they two shall be one flesh.
This is a great mystery: but
I speak concerning
Christ and the church.
Eph. 5:31,32

15.   Ephesians 5:29,30
For no man ever yet hated
his own flesh;   but
nourisheth and cherisheth it,
even as the Lord the church:
For we are members
of **his** body,
of **his** flesh,   and
of **his** bones.
Eph. 5:29,30

16.   Romans 7:4
Wherefore, my brethren,
ye also are become dead to the law
by the body of Christ;   that
ye should be married to another,
even to **him**
who is raised from the dead,   that
we should bring forth fruit unto God.
Rom. 7:4

13.   Genesis 1:27; 2:24
S G c m   i **h** o i,
i t i o G   c **h** h;
m a f c   **h** t.
T s m l
h f a h m,   a
c u h w: a
t s b o f.
Addr.____

14.   Ephesians 5:31,32
F t c s a m l
h f a m,   a
s b j u h w,   a
t t s b o f.
T i a g m: b
I s c
C a t c.
Addr.____

15.   Ephesians 5:29,30
F n m e y h
h o f;   b
n a c i,
e a t L t c:
F w a m
o **h** b,
o **h** f,   a
o **h** b.
Addr.____

16.   Romans 7:4
W, m b,
y a a b d t t l
b t b o C;   t
y s b m t a,
e t **h**
w i r f t d,   t
w s b f f u G.
Addr.____

17.   Ephesians 5:25b-27
Christ also loved the church,   and
gave **himself** for it;   That
he might sanctify   and cleanse it with
the washing of water by the word,   That
he might present it to **himself**
a glorious church, not having spot,   or
wrinkle,   or any such thing;   but that
it should be holy   and without blemish.
Eph. 5:25b-27

17.   Ephesians 5:25b-27
C a l t c,   a
g **h** f i;   T
h m s   a c i w
t w o w b t w, T
h m p i t **h**
a g c, n h s,   o
w, o a s t;   b t
i s b h   a w b.
Addr.____

18.   Matthew 22:2,8,10-12a
The kingdom of heaven is like
unto a certain king,
which made a marriage for his son,
Then saith he to his servants,
The wedding is ready,   but
they which were bidden were not worthy.
So those servants went out into the highways,   and
gathered together all as many as they found,
both bad and good: and
the wedding was furnished with guests.   And
when the king came in to see the guests,
he saw there a man which had not on
a wedding garment:
he saith unto him,
Friend, how camest thou in hither
not having a wedding garment?
Mt. 22:2,8,10-12a

18.   Matthew 22:2,8,10-12a
T k o h i l
u a c k,
w m a m f h s,
T s h t h s,
T w i r,   b
t w w b w n w.
S t s w o i t h,   a
g t a a m a t f,
b b a g: a
t w w f w g.   A
w t k c i t s t g,
h s t a m w h n o
a w g:
h s u h,
F, h c t i h
n h a w g?
Addr.____

19.   1 Corinthians 1:29,30
That no flesh should glory
in **his** presence.   But
of **him** are ye in Christ Jesus,
who of God is made unto us
wisdom,   and
righteousness,   and
sanctification,   and
redemption:
1 Cor. 1:29,30

19.   1 Corinthians 1:29,30
T n f s g
i **h** p.   B
o **h** a y i C J,
w o G i m u u
w,   a
r,   a
s,   a
r:
Addr.____

20.   Matthew 25:1,5-10
Then shall the kingdom of heaven be likened
unto ten virgins, which took their lamps, and
went forth to meet the bridegroom.
While the bridegroom tarried,
they all slumbered and slept.   And
at midnight there was a cry made,
Behold, the bridegroom cometh;
go ye out to meet him.
Then all those virgins arose ...   And
the foolish said unto the wise,
[The wise had oil with them.] Give us of your oil;
for our lamps are gone out.   But
the wise answered, saying, Not so;
lest there be not enough ...   And
while they [the foolish] went to buy,
the bridegroom came;   and
they that were ready
went in with him to the marriage: and
the door was shut.
Mt. 25:1,5-10

20.   Matthew 25:1,5-10
T s t k o h b l
u t v, w t t l,   a
w f t m t b.
W t b t,
t a s a s.   A
a m t w a c m,
B, t b c;
g y o t m h.
T a t v a ...   A
t f s u t w,
G u o y o;
f o l a g o.   B
t w a, s, N s;
l t b n e ...   A
w t w t b,
t b c;   a
t t w r
w i w h t t m: a
t d w s.
Addr._____

21.   Luke 10:25,26a,29-34a,36,37
... a certain lawyer ... tempted **him** [Jesus], saying,
Master, what shall I do to inherit eternal life?
[Jesus] He said unto him, What is written in the law?
But he, willing to justify himself [quoted the two
greatest commandments], unto Jesus,   And
[said] who is my neighbour?   And
Jesus answering ...   a certain priest ... passed by ...
likewise a Levite ...   passed by ... Luke 10:30b,33
a certain man ...   wounded ... and ... half dead ...
a certain Samaritan ... came where he was ...
when he saw him,   he had compassion ... and
took care of him.
Which now of these three ...was neighbour unto him...?
And he said, He that shewed mercy on him.
Then said Jesus unto him [the lawyer],
Go, and do thou likewise.
Lk. 10:25,26a,29-34a,36,37

21.   Luke 10:25,26a,29-34a,36,37
... a c l ... t **h**, s,
M, w s I d t i e l?
H s u h, W i w i t l?
B h, w t j h,
u J,   A
w i m n?   A
J a ...   a c p ... p b ...
l a L ...   p b ...
a c m ...   w ... a ... h d ...
a c S ...   c w h w ...
w h s h,   h h c ... a
t c o h.
W n o t t ... w n u h ...?
A h s, H t s m o h.
T s J u h,
G, a d t l.
Addr._____

22.   Galatians 3:1,3
O foolish Galatians,
who hath bewitched you,   that
ye should   not obey the truth,
before whose eyes
Jesus Christ hath been evidently set forth,
crucified among you?
Are ye so foolish?
having begun in the Spirit,
are ye now made perfect
by the flesh?
Gal. 3:1,3

22.   Galatians 3:1,3
O f G,
w h b y,   t
y s   n o t t,
b w e
J C h b e s f,
c a y?
A y s f?
h b i t S,
a y n m p
b t f?
Addr._____

23.   1 Corinthians 15:50,51
Now this I say, brethren,   that
flesh and blood cannot inherit
the kingdom of God;
neither doth corruption
inherit incorruption.
Behold, I shew you a mystery;
We shall not all sleep,   but
we shall all be changed,
1 Cor. 15:50,51

23.   1 Corinthians 15:50,51
N t I s, b,   t
f a b c i
t k o G;
n d c
i i.
B, I s y a m;
W s n a s, b
w s a b c,
Addr._____

24.   Matthew 25:13
Watch therefore,   for ye know
neither the day   nor the hour wherein
the Son of **man** cometh.
Mt. 25:13

24.   Matthew 25:13
W t,   f y k
n t d   n t h w
t S o **m** c.
Addr._____

25.   Genesis 1:28
And God blessed them,   and God said unto them,
Be fruitful, and multiply, and
replenish the earth,   and
subdue it: and have dominion
over the fish of the sea,   and
over the fowl of the air,   and
over every living thing   that
moveth upon the earth.
Gen. 1:28

25.   Genesis 1:28
A G b t,   a G s u t,
B f, a m,   a
r t e,   a
s i: a h d
o t f o t s,   a
o t f o t a,   a
o e l t   t
m u t e.
Addr._____

26.   Genesis 1:29,30
And God said, Behold,
I have given you
every herb bearing seed,   which is
upon the face of all the earth,   and
every tree, in the which
is the fruit of a tree   yielding seed;
to you it shall be for meat.   And
to every beast of the earth,   and
to every fowl of the air,   and
to every thing that creepeth   upon the earth,
wherein there is life,
I have given every green herb
for meat: and it was so.
Gen. 1:29,30

26.   Genesis 1:29,30
A G s, B,
I h g y
e h b s,   w i
u t f o a t e,   a
e t, i t w
i t f o a t   y s;
t y i s b f m.   A
t e b o t e,   a
t e f o t a,   a
t e t t c   u t e,
w t i l,
I h g e g h
f m: a i w s.
Addr.____

27.   John 6:51
[Jesus said] I am the living bread ...   and
the bread   that
I ... give is **my** flesh,
which I ... give for the life
of the world.
Jn. 6:51

27.   John 6:51
I a t l b ... a
t b   t
I ... g i **m** f,
w I ... g f t l
o t w.
Addr.____

28.   John 12:26
If any man serve **me**,
let him   follow **me**;   and
where I am,
there shall also **my** servant be:
if any man serve **me**,
him will **my** Father honour.
Jn. 12:26

28.   John 12:26
I a m s **m**,
l h   f **m**; a
w I a,
t s a m s b:
i a m s **m**,
h w **m** F h.
Addr.____

29.   Genesis 1:31
**And God saw every thing   that
he had made,   and, behold,
it was very good.**   And
the evening   and the morning
were the sixth day.
Gen. 1:31

29.   Genesis 1:31
**A G s e t   t
h h m,   a, b,
i w v g.**   A
t e   a t m
w t s d.
Addr.____

DAY SEVEN: ANALOGY SYNOPSIS

On Day Seven,
God rested from His work. Creation is finished.
God blessed the seventh day and sanctified it.

This reminds me that Jesus rested from His work;
the sacrifice is finished. He blessed the whole world
for He secured "the way" of direct access to Holy
God, and the sanctification of His disciples.

Jesus Christ glorified His Father on earth, and in
heaven Father God glorified His Son – the victorious
Lamb – the true Light.

ANALOGY: GOD RESTED

God's Work of Creation Is Finished. Jesus' Work, to Die to Save Sinners, Is Finished; He Lives.

Day 7: Genesis 2:1-3

1 Thus the heavens and the earth were finished, and all the host of them. 2 And on the seventh day God ended his work which he had made; and he rested on the seventh day from all his work which he had made. 3 And God blessed the seventh day, and sanctified it: because that in it he had rested from all his work which God created and made.

God's Work in Creation: Done: God is finished. He rested on the seventh day.

Jesus' Work on Earth: Done: Jesus Christ is finished; He died on the cross for our sins and paid our penalty of death – once for all. Before His crucifixion, Jesus secured from His Father, the perfect Counselor and Helper for His disciples – the Holy Spirit. Thereby once resurrected, the Lord Jesus Christ sat down at His Father's right hand – at rest from His atoning work on earth.

Bible Verse Keywords: Thus the heavens and the earth ... were finished; the seventh day God ended his work; he rested; It is finished; was risen early on the first day of the week; he was received up into heaven; sat on the right hand of God;

Pondered:

1. The heavens and the earth were finished, and God rested from all His work. He blessed the seventh day and sanctified it. The sentence of death for every man, woman, and child was paid; "It is finished." Jesus is at rest from all His sacrificial, substitutionary work.

2. Hebrews 10:14 says, "For by one offering he hath perfected for ever them that are sanctified." "Christ also loved the church, and gave himself for it; That he might sanctify and cleanse it with the washing of water by the word," declares Ephesians 5:25b,26. Jesus, Who knew no sin, bore our sins, so we might become His righteousness before His Holy Father.

3. Jesus said to His Father in John 17:4,5, **"I have glorified thee on the earth: I have finished the work which thou gavest me to do. And now, O Father, glorify thou me with thine own self with the glory which I had with thee before the world was."**

4. Thus the resurrected Jesus Christ was carried up to heaven and received by His Father. Christ sat down at His Father's right hand.

5. With the return of His Son – the victorious Mediator, God sent the Holy Spirit – the Counselor Helper. Now He is at work on earth drawing people to Jesus, indwelling believers, sanctifying and filling them, speaking and teaching of Christ, and empowering disciples to be like their Savior Lord.

6. The Lord Jesus Christ is at work in heaven preparing a place for each disciple transformed by His finished cross work and His Lordship.

DAY 7:   LIVING HOPE

1.   Genesis 2:1-3
Thus the heavens and the earth
were finished,   and
all the host of them.   And
on the seventh day
God ended **his** work
which **he** had made;   and
he rested on
the seventh day
from all **his** work
which **he** had made.   And

God blessed the seventh day,   and
sanctified it:
because that in it
he had rested from all **his** work
which God created and made.
Gen. 2:1-3

2.   John 19:28a,30b; Luke 23:46b
After this, Jesus knowing   that
all things
were now accomplished,   that
the scripture might be fulfilled ...
he said, It is finished ...Lk. 23:46b and
gave up the ghost.
Jn. 19:28a,30b; Lk. 23:46b

3.   Mark 16:9a,14a,19b; Luke 24:50b,51
Now when Jesus was risen early
the first day of the week ...
he appeared unto the eleven ... Lk. 24:50b,51
he lifted up **his** hands,   and
blessed them.   And
it came to pass, while **he** blessed them,
he was parted from them,   and
carried up into heaven. Mark 16:19b
he was received up into heaven,   and
sat on the right hand of God.
Mk. 16:9a,14a,19b; Lk. 24:50b,51

MEDITATION SCRIPTURES

1.   Genesis 2:1-3
T t h a t e
w f,   a
a t h o t.   A
o t s d
G e h w
w **h** h m;   a
h r o
t s d
f a **h** w
w **h** h m.   A

G b t s d,   a
s i:
b t i i
h h r f a **h** w
w G c a m.
Addr._____

2.   John 19:28a,30b; Luke 23:46b
A t, J k   t
a t
w n a,   t
t s m b f ...
h s, I i f ...   a
g u t g.
Addr._____

3. Mark 16:9a,14a,19b; Luke 24:50b,51
N w J w r e
t f d o t w ...
h a u t e ...
h l u **h** h,   a
b t.   A
i c t p, w **h** b t,
h w p f t,   a
c u i h.
h w r u i h, a
s o t r h o G.
Addr._____

4.   Colossians 1:19,20
For it pleased the Father   that
in **him** [Jesus] should all fulness dwell;   And,
having made peace
through the blood of **his** cross,
by **him**   to reconcile all things
unto **himself**;   by **him** ...
whether they be things in earth,   or
things in heaven.
Col. 1:19,20

4.   Colossians 1:19,20
F i p t F   t
i **h** s a f d;   A,
h m p
t t b o **h** c,
b **h**   t r a t
u **h**;   b **h** ...
w t b t i e,   o
t i h.
Addr.____

5.   1 Timothy 2:5,6a
For there is one God,   and
one **mediator** between God   and men,
the **man** Christ Jesus;
Who gave **himself**
a ransom for all
1 Tim. 2:5,6a

5.   1 Timothy 2:5,6a
F t i o G,   a
o **m** b G   a m,
t **m** C J;
W g **h**
a r f a
Addr.____

6.   1 Peter 1:3,4
Blessed be the God and Father
of our Lord Jesus Christ,
which according to **his** abundant mercy
hath begotten us again
unto a lively hope
by the resurrection of Jesus Christ
from the dead,
To an inheritance incorruptible,   and
undefiled,   and that
fadeth not away,
reserved in heaven for you,
1 Pet. 1:3,4

6.   1 Peter 1:3,4
B b t G a F
o o L J C,
w a t **h** a m
h b u a
u a l h
b t r o J C
f t d,
T a i i, a
u,   a t
f n a,
r i h f y,
Addr.____

7.   1 John 4:9
In this was manifested
the love of God toward us,   because that
God sent **his** only begotten Son
into the world,   that
we might live through **him**.
1 Jn. 4:9

7.   1 John 4:9
I t w m
t l o G t u,   b t
G s **h** o b S
i t w,   t
w m l t **h**.
Addr.____

8.   Romans 15:13
Now the God of hope
fill you with all joy   and
peace in believing,   that
ye may abound in hope,
through the power of the Holy Ghost.
Rom. 15:13

8.   Romans 15:13
N t G o h
f y w a j a
p i b,   t
y m a i h,
t t p o t H G.
Addr._____

9.   Romans 1:20a
For the invisible things of **him**
from the creation of the world
are clearly seen,
being understood by the things   that
are made,
even **his** eternal power   and
Godhead ...
Rom. 1:20a

9.   Romans 1:20a
F t i t o **h**
f t c o t w
a c s,
b u b t t t
a m,
e **h** e p a
G ...
Addr._____

10.   John 1:9
That was the true Light,
which lighteth every man   that
cometh into the world.
Jn. 1:9

10.   John 1:9
T w t t L,
w l e m t
c i t w.
Addr._____

11.   Revelation 21:2
And I [Apostle] John saw
the holy city, new Jerusalem,
coming down from God out of heaven,
prepared as a bride
adorned for her **husband**.
Rev. 21:2

11.   Revelation 21:2
A I J s
t h c, n J,
c d f G o o h,
p a a b
a f h **h**.
Addr._____

12.   Revelation 21:23
And the city had no need
of the sun, neither of the moon,
to shine in it:
for the glory of God
did lighten it,   and
the Lamb is the light ...
Rev. 21:23

12.   Revelation 21:23
A t c h n n
o t s, n o t m,
t s i i:
f t g o G
d l i, a
t L i t l ...
Addr._____

EPILOGUE: THE ESSENTIALS

HOW TO BE SAVED / RECEIVE CHRIST IN YOUR HEART

Holy God Creator,

I, _____, on _____ __, 2____.
       (name)   (date)

Admit that I am a sinner, and I deserve Your penalty of death for sin. I am sorry for my sins, and sincerely ask you to forgive me.

I:

Believe that Jesus Christ is Your Son and God. He paid my penalty of death when He died on the cross for my sins. He rose on the third day; therefore, I am assured that the penalty for my sin was paid and accepted. My forgiveness is only through faith in Jesus' sacrifice for me.

I:

Confess that I have received Your gift of forgiveness, and desire You to control my life. Now I am *a child of God.* I am an imitator of Jesus Christ empowered by God to turn away from sin and live victoriously for Christ. I am *a believer, saved, an heir of God with eternal life.* **Now Jesus Christ is my Lord, Master, and Savior.**

LORDSHIP: TWO GREATEST COMMANDMENTS

... Jesus answered ...

And thou shalt love the Lord thy God

with all thy heart, and

with all thy soul, and

with all thy mind, and

with all thy strength:

this is the first commandment.

And the second is like,

namely this,

Thou shalt love thy neighbour

as thyself.

There is none other commandment

greater than these.
Mark 12:29-31

THE HOLY BIBLE: THE LIVING WORD OF GOD

For the word of God is quick, and powerful, and sharper than any twoedged sword, piercing even to the dividing asunder of soul and spirit, and of the joints and marrow, and is a discerner of the thoughts and intents of the heart. Neither is there any creature that is not manifest in his sight: but all things are naked and opened unto the eyes of him with whom we have to do. Hebrews 4:12,13

If in reading this book, you prayed and received Jesus Christ into your heart as your Savior and Lord, please tell us.